Payments Systems in the U.S.

A Guide for the Payments Professional

CAROL COYE BENSON
SCOTT LOFTESNESS
RUSS JONES

THIRD EDITION

The answers you need about payments systems:

What are they?

Where did they come from?

How do they work?

Who uses them?

Who provides them?

Who profits from them?

How are they changing?

GLENBROOK PAYMENTS EDUCATION

This book is part of Glenbrook Partners' Payments Industry Education Program: a series of workshops, books, articles, webinars and research reports for payments professionals. The program includes Glenbrook's popular Payments Boot Camp, which has been attended by over 14,000 payments professionals since 2005.

GLENBROOK PRESS

Glenbrook Partners, LLC
535 Mission Street – 14th Floor
San Francisco, CA 94105
www.glenbrook.com

Ordering Information: Special discounts are available on quantity purchases. For details, contact the publisher at the address above or via email: books@glenbrook.com

Kindle edition: ISBN 978-0-9827897-5-9
Third edition (print only): ISBN 978-0-9827897-4-2

About the Authors

Carol Coye Benson's practice at Glenbrook focuses on mobile payments, national infrastructures, and emerging technologies for financial services. Before founding Glenbrook Partners, Carol was a managing director of the Global Institutional Services division of Deutsche Bank, leading marketing, client online services, and Internet development. At Visa International, she led groups working on eCommerce card security, database marketing, and technology investments. Also with Visa International, Carol founded and managed a European product development office, where she managed a series of eCommerce and chip card projects for banks across Europe. Earlier, Carol spent twelve years with Citibank, where she managed the development and market introduction of new commercial payments products. Carol began her career as a corporate lending officer for large multinationals at both Bank of America and Citibank.

Email Carol: carol@glenbrook.com
LinkedIn: www.linkedin.com/in/carolcoyebenson

Scott Loftesness, works with major clients as well as financial services startups and investors, helping with the refinement of business models, approaches to technical design, and go-to-market strategies. With over 45 years of experience in information technology—as a technologist, senior executive, board member, venture investor, consultant, advisor, and mentor—Scott brings a unique business and technology perspective to his work with Glenbrook. Earlier in his career, Scott was group executive vice president at First Data Merchant Services. Scott also served as group executive vice president at Visa International, where he led the development of Visa's global payment systems strategies, including Visa's research and development initiatives related to card payments, eCommerce payments and advanced card technologies. Scott began his career as a systems engineer with IBM in San Francisco.

Email Scott: scott@glenbrook.com
LinkedIn: www.linkedin.com/in/scottloftesness

Russ Jones manages Glenbrook's Payments Boot Camp Program. He is an industry pioneer in the commercial use of Internet technologies, and has a strong background in payments industry analysis, strategy development, and product conceptualization. Before joining Glenbrook, Russ was a general partner with The NuVantage Group, an innovation-to-market consulting group, where his clients included CommerceNet and the Financial Services Technology Consortium. Earlier, Russ served as director of emerging technologies for Digital Equipment's corporate research group in Palo Alto.

Email Russ: russ@glenbrook.com
LinkedIn: www.linkedin.com/in/gprussjones

Why We Wrote This Book!

Glenbrook Partners is a leading strategy consulting firm in the payments industry. When we started the firm, we realized that executives from many of our clients (banks, processors, networks, technology and service providers, as well as merchants, payments/fintech startups and investors) wanted a more in-depth understanding of how the U.S. payments systems actually work.

In response to this, we developed the Glenbrook Payments Boot Camp—a two-day "deep dive" into the U.S. payments industry—covering value chains, economics, regulation, products, markets, risk management and technology. Over 14,000 payments professionals have attended this unique program since it was launched in 2005.

Payments Systems in the U.S. draws on this material—and explains, in clear and simple language, how this industry works, who makes money from it, and how it is changing. We also share some of the historical perspective on the industry to help readers better appreciate some of the interesting twists and turns that took place in the industry's evolution.

Thanks!

We want to thank our other partners: Allen Weinberg, Bryan Derman, Erin McCune, Elizabeth McQuerry, George Peabody, and Beth Horowitz Steel. We dedicate this book to the late Dennis Moser, our longtime Glenbrook partner who helped spur us on to creating Glenbrook's Payments Education Program.

Thanks as well to our many clients and friends in the industry, who work on bringing innovation to payments and making it the exciting business it is!

Share your feedback!

We welcome your feedback on this book—just send us an email and we'll get back to you! Email: books@glenbrook.com

Table of Contents

Table of Figures

Table of Tables

Introduction

PAYMENTS ARE A BIG part of all of our lives. We pay for things we want and need. We scramble for change in our purse or pockets; we shuffle through the cards in our wallet to find the right one for a purchase. We write checks or pay bills online. We buy gift cards and schedule mortgage payments. We buy things online or with our mobile phones, and try various cards and wallets for payment. We send money to friends and family. We worry about funding big purchases; we try to find the right path for ordinary purchases. We're all different. For some of us, convenience is king; for others, control, or the collection of rewards, or following the patterns our parents taught us, determine how and why we make payments.

As businesspeople, we may be involved in how our businesses make payments—to employees, to suppliers, to governments. We may also be involved in how our businesses collect payments—from consumers or from businesses.

These activities are central to our personal and business lives. And for some of us, they are also the services that fuel our livelihoods. "Under the hood" of these simple payment transactions are the systems, products, and companies that form the payments industry.

This book is written for the *payments professional*. Payments professionals may work for companies that enable payments transactions. This includes banks, of course, but also many other types of companies—processors, payments services, software companies, point of sale terminal manufacturers, service providers, risk managers, and others. Some of these companies are powerful incumbents, while others are their competitors—startups that are bringing innovation to the industry. Many of these fail or stagnate, but a few succeed—and join the incumbents watching nervously for the next round of new challengers. Other payments professionals are responsible within an enterprise for the collection or disbursement of payments. Still others work as advisors, consultants, lawyers, or investors in the industry.

As in any industry, the professionals in the payments industry struggle to keep up with changes in the environment, in technology, and in the payments behavior of consumers, merchants, and other users of payments systems. Some payments professionals are well-versed in one payments system (Cards, perhaps, or ACH); others in a function such as consumer marketing or risk management. This book provides a comprehensive view of the entire U.S. payments industry, including all its systems and functions.

This book is not a source for statistics or "league tables" on payments. There are many such industry sources: at the end of each chapter we include a list of resources that offer more information about a particular payments system or topic.

We have tried to be as unbiased as possible; any opinions, speculations, or anecdotes on a topic are set in shaded boxes. We very much welcome your questions and comments. Email us: **books@glenbrook.com** and we'll respond!

Payments
Systems
Overview

WHAT IS A PAYMENT? A payment is the transfer of value from one end party—the Sender—to another—the Receiver.

A payment is a transfer of value

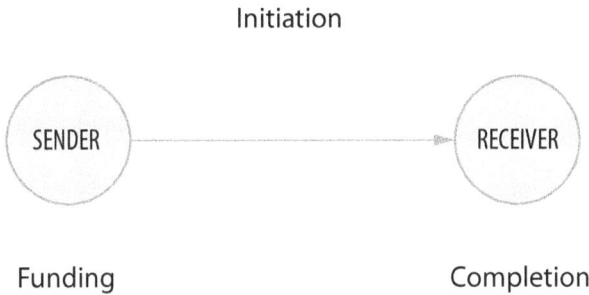

Initiation

(SENDER) - - - - - - - ▷ (RECEIVER)

Funding   Completion

*Figure 2-1: Payment
is a Transfer of Value*

This transfer of value is denominated in currency—almost always, in the national currency of the payments system being used. We think of three elements involved in a payments transfer: the initiation of the payment, the funding of the payment by the sender, and the delivery of payment to the receiver. In some payment systems, the receiver initiates the payments. In others, it is the sender's responsibility. The elapsed time from initiation to completion could be several seconds, or it might be four to seven business days. It depends on the system.

A payments system, as shown in the figure below, defines how such value transfers are done and provides a framework of rules for users of the system.

A payment system may be centralized, decentralized, or "virtual."
A payment system connects large numbers of end parties,
formalizes processes for transfer of value, and plays some role in
managing risks for the participants.

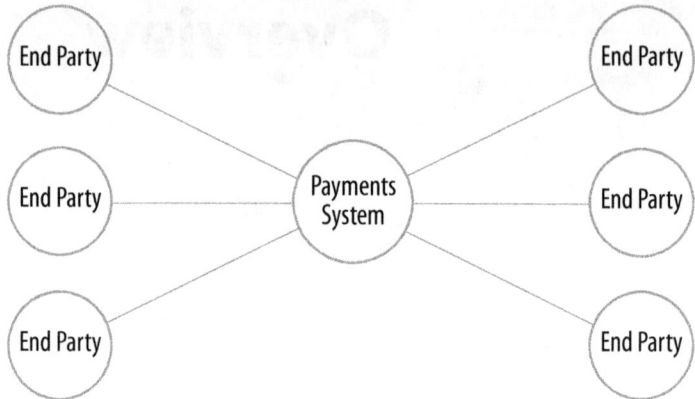

Figure 2-2: What is a
Payment System?

There are many types of payments systems. Most share these common characteristics:

- Operate within a single country on a national basis within that country.

- Are denominated in the currency of that country.

- Are subject, directly or indirectly, to regulation by the government of that country.

- Enable multiple parties to transact with each other.

Payments System Models

Payments systems can operate on a variety of models. The two most common models are referred to as the "open loop" model and the "closed loop" model. There are also hybrid models that have some of the characteristics found in open loop systems and some of the characteristics found in closed loop systems.

Open Loop Systems

Open loop systems operate on a hub-and-spoke model. Almost all large-scale payments systems use this model. An open loop system requires intermediaries (almost always banks or depository financial institutions) to join the payments system. These intermediaries then form business relationships with end parties (consumers or merchants, for example).

An open loop payments system relies on intermediaries, usually banks, to connect end parties.

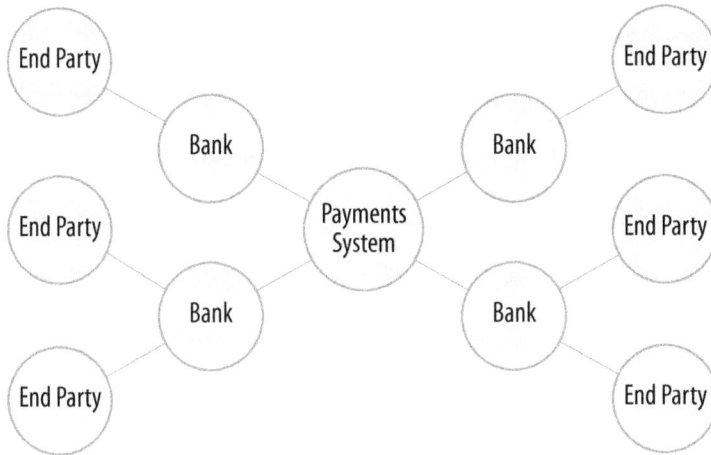

Figure 2-3: Open Loop Systems

A transaction is passed from one end party to his or her bank, on to the payments system, on to the other end party's bank, and then on to that end party. This structure allows the two end parties to transact with each other without having direct relationships with each other's banks. The banks, similarly, can transact with each other without a direct relationship.

Today, most electronic payments systems—both paper-based and electronic (cards, ACH, wire transfers and even check images)—operate on this model. This is true despite the fact that current technology would quite easily permit the exchange of electronic transactions on a bilateral basis. But, as we will see, the open loop model also creates an effective means of allocating liability.

The advantage of the open loop structure is that it allows a payments system to scale quite rapidly. As intermediaries join the payments system, all of their end party customers are immediately accessible to other intermediaries participating in the payments system.

In an open loop payments system, the network defines the operating rules to its participating banks who then must ensure compliance by their end parties—creating a chain of liability as shown below:

Other Terms in Open Loop Payments Systems

On-us transactions occur when the bank intermediary is the same on both sides of a transaction. Depending on the payments system, the transaction may stay within the bank (e.g., never be submitted to a clearing house or "hub" for switching), in which case the bank settles the transaction through an internal book transfer. In other systems, an on-us transaction is passed through the system and returns to the bank, just like a regular "off-us" transaction. The growing concentration of U.S. banks is increasing the percentage of "on-us" transactions.

Correspondent banking relationships between banks allow smaller banks, which may not participate directly in a payments system, to access that system on behalf of their customers through a relationship with a participant bank. Many smaller banks in the United States gain access to the wire transfer systems in this way. This model is also used extensively for cross-border payments.

A chain of liability allows rapid scaling of a global system

Network rules pass liability with the transaction—each party warrants compliance to the next. Banks pass on the liability to their customers.

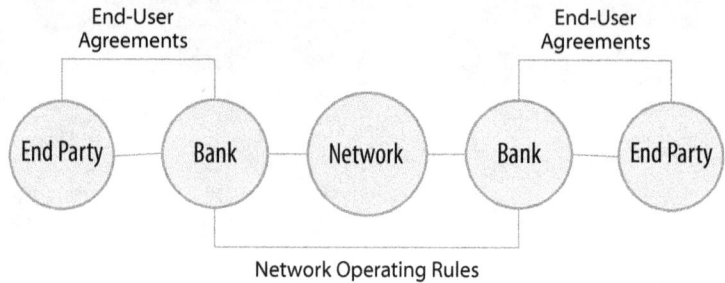

Figure 2-4: The Chain of Liability

> ### Open Loop Systems and the Chain of Liability
>
> In open loop systems, intermediaries and the network assume certain liabilities for the actions of their customers, as well as for their own actions. The nature and extent of these liabilities is determined by the operating rules of the payments system, and, in some circumstances, by national law and regulation.
>
> In the ACH system, for example, the originating bank of an ACH debit transaction warrants that its customer has properly obtained the consumer's consent for the debit to his or her account. If the consumer successfully disputes a transaction, the originating bank must reimburse the consumer's bank.
>
> The originating bank will, of course, try to recoup this from its customer—but if unsuccessful, the bank is left "holding the bag." Similarly, in the card networks, if a customer initiates a dispute that (according to the rules) requires a transaction to be reversed, the merchant's acquiring bank is ultimately responsible to the network for the obligation of its merchant customer.

Closed Loop Systems

A closed loop payments system operates without intermediaries. The end parties have a direct relationship with the payments system. The original American Express and Discover systems, and the proprietary card systems (for example, a Macy's credit card accepted only at Macy's) are examples of closed loop systems. Most payments services providers operate as closed loop systems, although some may access open loop systems for transaction funding or delivery.

Closed loop systems have the advantage of simplicity. As one entity sets all of the rules and has a direct relationship with the end parties, it can act more quickly and more flexibly than the distributed open loop systems, which must propagate change throughout the system's intermediary layers. The disadvantage of closed loop systems is that they are more difficult to grow than open loop systems; the payments system must sign up each end party individually.

As we will see in Chapter 5 (Cards), some of the closed loop card payments systems are in the process of evolving toward more open loop models.

Payments services providers, such as PayPal or Western Union, operate closed loop systems. But it is important to note that these providers themselves are users of the open loop systems, often on an aggregated basis. They use the open loop systems to fund transactions from senders and/or to deliver payment to the receiving party.

Payments Systems in the United States

There are five core payments systems in the United States:

- Cash

- The checking system

- The card systems (charge, credit, debit and prepaid cards)

- The ACH (Automated Clearing House) system

- The wire transfer systems

As we will see in our discussion on payments innovation later in Chapter 10, there are many other ways of making payments, including methods such as online banking/bill payment and products such as email and mobile telephone payments services. Almost all of these methods rely on one or more of the core payments systems to actually transfer value between parties—using them for the funding and completion steps described earlier. As we write this book, the United States is in the process, along with many other countries, of instituting a new "sixth rail" payments system—the so-called "immediate funds transfer", or "faster payments" system.

> ### Origins: Check Clearing Houses
>
> Initially formed in the 1800s, check clearing houses were the first large-scale open loop systems in the United States. Before clearing houses existed, each bank receiving a deposit containing a check drawn on another bank needed to present that check directly to the check writer's bank in order to collect payment on it.
>
> As the volume of checks in use rose, this required a complex web of bilateral relationships among banks in a city. Clearing a check drawn on a bank in another city was even more complicated, and often required one or more correspondent banks to effect payment.
>
> The earliest check clearing house was a simple meeting, each business morning, of representatives from each participating bank in a city. Clerks from each of the banks would come to the clearing house bearing bags of checks. At the clearing house, the checks would be exchanged and each clerk would depart with the checks written on accounts at his bank. (It is interesting to note that in the early phases of the card industry, paper "sales drafts" were cleared in much the same way.) Below is an example of a clearing house from 1883.
>
>

Payments System Volumes

Payments system volumes are measured in two ways: by count and amount. "Count" refers to the number of transactions processed, and "amount" to the total dollar value of those transactions. (Note: other sources, in the card systems in particular, use the term "volume" to refer to the amount, or the aggregate dollar value of the transactions.)

Some systems do a better job of measuring themselves than others. The wire transfer systems and some card systems, for example, have quite precise measures. But checking, and especially cash, have no formal mechanisms for precise national measurement, and are therefore simply estimated. The Federal Reserve Bank of Boston conducts a "Survey of Consumer Payment Choice" which periodically surveys several thousand U.S. consumers on their use of various payments system. This survey breaks out consumer usage of card types between credit cards, debit cards, and prepaid cards.

The table below shows Glenbrook's estimates for U.S. payments systems volumes as a percent of total payments systems transactions for the year 2015.

System	Count (MM)	Amount ($B)	Avg. Value ($)
Debit Cards	74,210	$2,313	$31.26
Credit Cards	30,771	$2,832	$92.03
Subtotal Cards	104,981	$5,145	$49.00
ACH	24,000	$41,700	$1,737.50
Checks	13,700	$21,458	$1,566.29
Cash	67,150	$1,410	$21.00
Totals	209,830	$69,713	

Table 2-1: U.S. Payments Systems Volumes. Source: Glenbrook analysis for 2015. Excludes wire transfer; cash estimate is consumer use.

Note that wire transfers are excluded. If wire transfers had been included, wire transfers would represent less than 1% of the total "count", but 93% of the total "amount"—because of the high-value financial market transactions that use wire transfers. The totals shown are large—much larger than the U.S. Gross National Product. This is because a single commercial transaction (such as a consumer purchase) can result in multiple payments, as the various parties in the value chain move funds to effect payment, settlement, etc.

Payments System Functions

Payments systems must provide three key functions: processing, rules, and brand. Some payments systems provide all three functions through a single organization. Others accommodate these functions via a virtual, or distributed model.

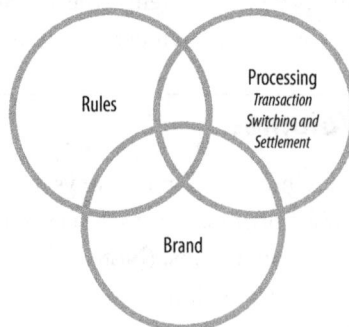

Figure 2-5: Payment Systems Functions

Processing means switching—the way in which a transaction moves from one party to another. In a closed loop system, this transfers value between the end parties. In an open loop system, this transfers value between intermediaries on behalf of their end parties. As the term is used here, processing also includes settlement—the process by which intermediaries in an open loop system transfer value—usually on a net basis—to cover the individual transactions each has been a party to.

Rules (sometimes called "operating rules" or "operating regulations") bind each of the participants in a system. In an open loop system, the rules bind the intermediaries. Although the rules may require intermediaries to compel certain things of their end parties, the end parties are not directly bound by the rules. In a closed loop system, the rules bind the end parties directly.

Brand is the means by which the parties to a transaction communicate to each other how they will pay. This is sometimes branding with a "capital B" (e.g., "Do you take Mastercard?") and sometimes with a "small b" ("I'll give you a check.") For the card networks in particular, significant brand advertising has been an important driver of payments system growth.

The Domains of Payment

Payments are used, of course, for multiple purposes. We categorize these uses into six domains of payment, each of which exhibits unique characteristics and requirements:

- **Point of Sale (POS).** Payments made at the physical point of sale. Includes store and restaurant payments, but also unattended environments such as vending machines and transit kiosks. POS payments are sometimes referred to as proximity payments.

- **Remote commerce.** Payments made for purchases where the buyer is remote from the seller. This includes online and mobile purchasing, as well as mail-order or telephone-order buying. Key segments are eRetailing, online travel and entertainment, digital subscriptions, and digital content.

- **Bill payment.** Payments made by individuals or businesses based on receipt of a bill. This domain includes utilities, insurance, and services (personal or business) that are paid on a periodic, recurring basis.

- **P2P payment.** Person-to-person payments. Includes domestic payments among friends and families, but

Terminology

Throughout this book, we use the term "end party" to refer to both the receiver and the sender of funds. An end party may be a consumer, or may be a merchant or other enterprise—for example, a biller, small business, government, or non-profit. In any payment transaction, one end party is the payer, and one the receiver, of funds. As we will see, either the payer or the receiver may initiate the payment, depending on payments system and type.

We will use the term "provider" to refer to parties who are providing access to the payments systems to end users and/or other providers. Banks, networks, clearing houses, processors and service providers are all types of providers. Finally, we use the term "bank," unless otherwise noted, to refer to all depository financial institutions in the United States, including credit unions, thrifts, and savings banks.

We use the term "payments system" to refer to the set of providers who follow a common protocol and have common operating rules. A "payments network" refers to a specific organization that writes and maintains rules for its network. So we refer to the "card payments system" and to the "Mastercard payments network." In other countries, what we call a payments network is sometimes referred to as a "scheme."

also cross-border remittances (e.g., migrant workers sending money to relatives in home countries), and account-to-account transfers by individuals (referred to as "A2A" or, sometimes, "me to me" payments).

- **B2B payment.** Business-to-business payments. Includes payments from buyer to supplier, but also intracompany payments and, significantly, financial market payments (bank-to-bank payments, securities purchases, foreign exchange transactions, etc.). For the purposes of this framework, governments, non-profits, and other types of enterprises are included as "businesses."

- **Income payment.** Payments to individuals for salary, benefits, rebates, and expense reimbursements.

The payments systems support activity across these payments domains, and, in fact, compete with each other at a systems level.

A good example of this occurs in the B2B payments domain where checking, the traditional payments system used for business-to-business payments, is in decline. All of the electronic payments systems are competing for the B2B payments that have historically used checks. The ACH system has specialized transaction codes for B2B payments, and carries remittance data along with the payments. The card systems have business purchasing cards and small-business credit and debit card products. The wire transfer systems are enhancing their networks to carry remittance data to meet the requirements of this domain.

Meanwhile, the checking system itself, through imaging, remote deposit capture, and other advances, is competing to maintain volume.

Payments Systems Flow

The switching function in an open loop payments system is a message flow from the first intermediary to the network (which could be, in a centralized model, the payments system itself, or, in a distributed model, a hub or a clearing house) to the second intermediary. This message always flows in the same direction. What the message says, however, is different depending on whether the payment is a "push" or a "pull" payment.

While the concept of push and pull payments can be confusing, it is essential to understanding the workings of payments systems—in particular the risks and liabilities borne by the parties to a transaction.

"Push" or "pull" refers to the action of the party that is entering the transaction into the system. Push and pull payments are illustrated below:

The payment message flows the same way in both **push** and **pull** payments. In this diagram, End Party A is the party that enters a transaction into the payment system—for example, a merchant depositing a check or an employer sending a direct payroll deposit to its bank.

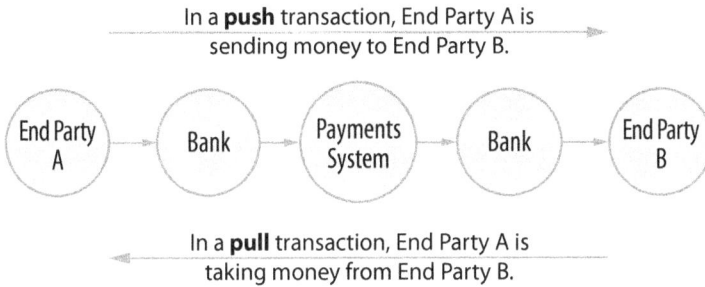

In a **push** transaction, End Party A is
sending money to End Party B.

End Party A → Bank → Payments System → Bank → End Party B

In a **pull** transaction, End Party A is
taking money from End Party B.

Figure 2-6: "Push" and "Pull" Transactions

- Any time that "End Party A" is sending money to "End Party B," it is considered a push payment—for example, a wire transfer or an ACH direct deposit of payroll. Using the direct deposit as an example, we see that the employer ("End Party A") is instructing its bank to send money to employees through the ACH network. In effect, the first bank is saying to the second bank, "I am debiting myself; you should credit yourself."

- When "End Party A" collects money from "End Party B," it is considered a pull payment. Checks, cards, and ACH debit transactions are pull payments. Using a check as an example, we see that the merchant ("End Party A") is, by depositing the check, instructing its bank to send that check through a clearing method to collect payment from "End Party B" (the check writer). In effect, the first bank is saying to the second bank, "I am crediting myself; you should debit yourself."

Given that push and pull payments involve different parties initiating a payment, it's worth understanding which end party needs to know what information to initiate a payment.

Who needs to know what in payments?

"Pull" Payments

The **payee** needs to know the bank and account number of the **payer**

Card account numbers and checks provide this to the payee

"Push" Payments

The **payer** needs to know the bank and account number of the **payee**

This is what a direct deposit of payroll form provides your employer

Figure 2-7: Who Needs to Know What in Payments?

"Push" payments are fundamentally much less risky than "pull" payments. In a "push" payment, the party who has funds is sending the money, so there is essentially no risk of NSF, or non-sufficient funds—"push" payments can't "bounce." Furthermore, in a "push" payments system the transaction is initiated by the sender's bank, which knows that its end party has the money. Other types of fraud, of course, are still possible.

"Pull" payments are inherently subject to "bouncing." The bank initiating the transaction does not know whether or not the bank receiving the transaction will be able to successfully apply that transaction to the credit or debit account of its customer. Furthermore, "pull" transactions depend on the payer ("End Party B") having authorized the "sender" of the message to effect the transaction. (A signed check presented to a merchant, or a card swipe with signature or PIN, are examples of such an authorization.)

Card networks are fundamentally "pull" payment networks. Card payments don't bounce—but this doesn't mean that they are push transactions. They are guaranteed "pull" transactions. The card networks accomplished this by adding a separate message flow, called the authorization, that runs through the network before the "pull" payment transaction is submitted. This authorization transaction asks, "Are there sufficient funds, or available credit balances, to pay this transaction?" If so, the "pull" transaction is submitted. Card network rules specify that merchants receiving this "yes" reply are covered for both insufficient funds and fraud risks. (Important differences in eCommerce and other environments in which the card is not present will be discussed in Chapters 5 and 8.)

Data Breaches in payments systems are typically the theft of payer account credentials (such as card numbers): the stolen credentials can be used to fraudulently "pull" money out of the account. In the card system, issuer tokenization is one important initiative to address this risk. But it is interesting to note that similar risks don't necessarily exist in a "push" system: if the payee's credentials can only be used to "push" money, then the theft of those credentials isn't harmful.

Payments System Settlement

Settlement in an open loop system refers to the process by which the intermediaries actually receive or send funds to each other. The settlement function in an open loop system can be done on either a net or a gross settlement basis:

- In a net settlement system, the net obligations of participating intermediaries are calculated by the payment system on a periodic basis—most typically daily. At the end of the day, a participating intermediary is given a net settlement total and instructed either (a) to fund a settlement account with that amount, should it be in a net debit position, or (b) that there are funds available to draw on in its settlement account, should it be in a net credit position.

Checking, card payments systems, and the ACH are all net settlement systems in the United States. For example, settlement of checks and ACH, when handled through a Federal Reserve bank, is done on a batch basis: a bank's account at a Federal Reserve Bank is periodically credited or debited with total amounts from a batch of transactions which have been processed.

The rules of the system specify whether, and to what extent, a participating bank may have an overdraft in their settlement account. This overdraft is a liability of the participating bank, and its failure to make good on the liability (if, for example, the bank goes out of business during the course of the settlement period) creates an obligation for the payments system: again, the rules of the system will specify how that obligation is handled.

- In a gross settlement system, each transaction settles as it is processed. With the Fedwire system, for example, a transaction is effected when the sending bank's account at a Federal Reserve Bank is debited and the receiving bank's account at a Federal Reserve Bank system is credited. No end-of-day settlement process is necessary in a gross settlement system.

Two kinds of settlement—how money actually moves!

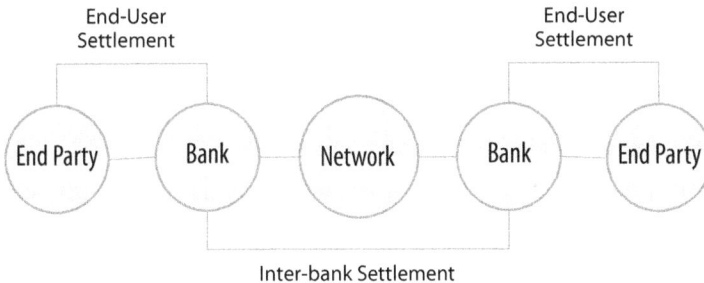

Inter-bank settlement in most open-loop systems is done on a net basis. The banks draw on or from their settlement accounts on a daily basis.

Figure 2-8: Two Kinds of Settlement—How Money Actually Moves!

How end party settlement is accomplished depends on the payments system. The timing and manner of a credit or debit to a consumer, merchant, or enterprise account may be defined by the payments system, by regulation, or simply by market practices between the bank and its end parties.

In a closed loop system, the only settlement is the end party settlement. The operator of the system defines how such a settlement is handled.

The Virtual Systems

Two core United States payments systems, cash and checking, operate on a virtual basis. By this we mean that there is no formal payments system that end parties, or bank intermediaries, "join."

We all know, of course, how cash works. The transaction is "switched" and "settled" directly between the two end parties. From that perspective, it is a push system. Other aspects of cash payments are covered in Chapter 6.

The checking system in the United States automatically includes all depository financial institutions—they do not have to "join." Banks do, however, usually join one or more clearing houses to switch and settle the checks they receive in deposits. The clearing houses have rules, but these are much more limited in scope than the rules of the card or ACH networks. In part, this is because U.S. law and regulation cover paper checks more extensively. Other aspects of checking are covered in Chapter 3.

These virtual systems have no "capital B" brand, and no central network that promotes their use.

Payments System Ownership and Regulation

Ownership

Most United States payments systems began as bank-owned systems. Over the past decade, as the table below shows, many of these payments systems have migrated to different ownership models. Some of the non-bank-owned payments systems are publicly traded companies; others are privately held.

Payments System	Original Owner	Current Owner
ACH*	Bank	Bank
American Express	Non-Bank	Non-Bank
Mastercard	Bank	Non-Bank
Visa	Bank	Non-Bank
Discover	Non-Bank	Non-Bank
STAR	Bank	Non-Bank
NYCE	Bank	Non-Bank
Fedwire**	Bank**	Bank**
CHIPS	Bank	Bank
Cash	None	None
Checking***	None	None

* The ACH operators are also indirectly bank-owned
** Fedwire is owner by the Federal Reserve Banks, which are in turn owned by the banks they serve.
*** Some check clearinghouses are bank-owned; some are owned by private sector processors.

Table 2-2: Payments System Ownership

Payments systems that are owned by large groups of banks tend to make rules that benefit the banks as a group. This can have the effect of "leveling the playing field"—all participating banks have equal access to products and services. Systems with large budgets for staff and advertising (notably the card networks) create fully defined products that the member banks then distribute to their customers. Systems with smaller budgets (such as the ACH) do much less in the way of product definition and management, and only provide the operating rules and/or platforms that the banks then use to create products.

Regulation

A mix of governmental and private rules regulates payments systems in the United States. Government rule, of course, is by law, and by regulations issued by agencies of the government to implement those laws. In the United States, the primary issuer of payments regulations is the Federal Reserve Board. Private rules can either take the form of network rules, or of simple contracts applying to a service used: the Federal Reserve Bank's operating circulars (governing the use of the Federal Reserve Bank payments services offered to banks) are an example of this. Private rules can be thought of as "agreement-based."

Private System Rules

Most payments systems require either intermediaries (open loop systems) or end parties (closed loop systems) to formally join the system. The party joining the system is bound by the rules of the system. In an open loop system, the intermediary's contract with its end party often contains provisions dictated by the operating rules, making the end parties indirectly governed by some of the rules. These operating rules are extremely important, particularly for open loop networks, as they define the parameters necessary for successful interoperability among thousands or millions of end parties.

Operating rules cover a wide range of topics, including:

- **Technical standards.** Data formats, token (e.g., card) specifications, delivery and receipt capabilities, data security standards, etc.

- **Processing standards.** Time limits for submitting and returning transactions, requirements for posting to end party accounts, etc.

- **Membership requirements.** Types of institutions that can join, capital requirements, etc.

- **Payment acceptance requirements.** Constraints on the ability to selectively accept payments transactions.

- **Exception processing and dispute resolution.** Rights and requirements of intermediaries and end parties, often with respect to disputing or refusing a transaction.

- **Fees.** Processing and other charges paid to the payments system; interchange, if any, among the intermediaries.

- **Brands and marks.** Standards for use of the payments system brand.

A new product at the payments system level (for example, contactless cards) or a new transaction type generally require a new set of operating rules that apply to that particular product or transaction type. Operating rules requirements can have significant financial impact on both users of and providers to a payments system. Investment may be required to meet technical standards or to provide certain forms of services, such as dispute resolution; changes in definition of liability or allocation of risk can also have large effects.

Some open loop payments systems, Visa, Mastercard, and NACHA (for ACH), make most of their operating rules publicly available on their websites. Other payments systems, such as CHIPS (for wire transfers) and most of the PIN debit card networks, do not make their operating rules available to non-members.

Changes to the operating rules of a payments system can be difficult and take years to implement. Most payments systems have several tiers of committees through which participants consider proposed rules changes. There is often a year or more of lag time between approval and implementation of a new rule.

The check payments system in the U.S., as discussed above, is a "virtual" system with no central authority. Banks do, however, join one or more check clearing houses to process checks. These clearing houses act like payments systems in that their operating rules bind the members. Such rules tend to be narrow in scope, however, compared to those in the card, ACH, and wire transfer systems. Check clearing house rules may specify times for presenting or returning items, image standards, etc.

United States Law and Federal Reserve Bank Regulation

U.S. law regulates some payments systems specifically, and others more generally. Federal Reserve Bank regulations implement law and specify requirements that are binding on the banks that they regulate. Key laws and regulations include:

- U.C.C. Article 3—Negotiable Instruments.

- U.C.C. Article 4—Bank Deposits and Collections.

- U.C.C. Article 4A—Funds Transfers.

- The Check Clearing for the 21st Century Act (Check 21).

- The Credit Card Accountability Responsibility and Disclosure Act of 2009.

- The Dodd-Frank Wall Street Reform and Consumer Protection Act of 2010, including the Durbin Amendment relating to U.S. debit card issuers and acquirers.

> ### Image Clearing and Regulatory Framework
>
> Today, banks, processors, and clearing houses are dealing with a complex regulatory framework following the dramatic shift to image clearing. For example, some regulations that apply to paper check clearing no longer apply to image clearing. This is a transitional period for the industry as it evaluates the right regulatory model for an all-image clearing world.

- Federal Reserve Bank Regulation E (implementing provisions in the Electronic Fund Transfer Act) applies to consumer electronic transactions including debit cards, ATM withdrawals, and ACH transactions (but not credit cards). Among other provisions, Regulation E establishes key consumer rights for repudiation and reversal of non-authorized transactions.

- Federal Reserve Bank Regulation CC—Availability of Funds and Collection of Checks.

- Federal Reserve Bank Regulation Z—Truth in Lending, prescribes uniform methods for computing the cost of credit, for disclosing credit terms, and for resolving errors on certain types of credit accounts.

- Federal Reserve Bank Regulation J—Collection of Checks and Other Items by Federal Reserve Banks and Funds Transfers through Fedwire, establishes procedures, duties, and responsibilities among (1) Federal

Reserve Banks, (2) the senders and payers of checks and other items, and (3) the senders and recipients of Fedwire funds transfers.

- Federal Reserve Bank Regulation II—limits the amount of debit card interchange for regulated (large) banks and specifies minimum routing options for debit card networks.

A number of other significant laws, regulations, and orders fall under the general category of bank regulation. These include regulation around money laundering, privacy, credit reporting, and other issues relevant to payments. Regulatory requirements around "Know Your Customer" (KYC) are particularly important for banks and non-banks in the payments industry. Provisions mandated by the Bank Secrecy Act and USA PATRIOT Act require a variety of identity checking procedures prior to opening a customer account.

State Banking Authorities

State law and regulations by state banking authorities apply mostly to non-bank providers of payments services, and are generally referred to as "money transmitter regulations." They regulate sales and issuance of payments instruments, as well as transmitting or receiving money. Almost every state now requires that money transmitters obtain a state license, post a bond, and/or maintain certain levels of net worth or permissible investments. Notably, state money transmission regulation is not uniform, creating additional challenges for payments companies with national ambitions. State banking authorities also regulate state-chartered banks.

> **The Future of Payments Regulation**
>
> It is interesting to reflect on what the future may hold for U.S. payments regulation. One can argue that the U.S. permits much more self-regulation of key payments systems than do other countries. This may be because banks in the U.S. are heavily regulated, by multiple authorities. The payments systems, historically owned by banks, were therefore de facto under a regulatory "umbrella." Today, many payments systems are no longer bank-owned. Does this mean that federal and other regulators may begin to take a more active role in the industry?

Economic Models for Payments Systems

Payments systems providers, including banks, networks, and processors, make money by providing access to payments systems for end parties. End parties include consumers, merchants, and enterprises (billers, other businesses, governments, and nonprofit groups). Processors and networks also make money by providing payments services to intermediaries such as banks. Many banks provide payments services to other banks as a part of correspondent banking relationships. Merchants may also provide payments services—for example, when they provide private-label or gift cards to consumers.

In this book, we will examine the economics of each core payments system, in turn, as we discuss each system. But a few general observations can be made about payments system economics:

- In both open loop and closed loop payments systems, providers have a direct business relationship with end party customers. Providers set prices for their services, as do other businesses. Providers realize revenue from payments through direct and indirect sources. This is true whether the end party is a consumer or an enterprise. Direct revenue comes from fees explicitly charged to the end party; these may include transaction fees, interest on associated loans, monthly maintenance fees, and exception fees (overdraft fees, bounced check fees, late payment fees). Indirect revenue comes from net interest income on deposit balances, float, and interchange.

- In some open loop payments systems, the rule-making body may define interchange for the system: a fee paid by one intermediary to the other in partial compensation for handling the transaction.

- Providers often price payments products as part of an overall bundle of services—for example, a checking account with bundled ATM access, checkwriting privileges, and a debit card. Similarly, a provider may price card acceptance services to a small merchant on a bundled price model—but may price the same service to a large merchant on an unbundled basis.

- Costs associated with providing payments services are a mix of fixed and variable costs. Typically, payments system providers have very high fixed costs and very low incremental costs for each transaction. A bank, for example, needs to cover the costs of staffing and maintaining a branch, engaging the service that replenishes its ATMs, and working with a check processing center. While unit costs may be calculated (add up the expenses and divide by the number of transactions), they are not always accurate indicators of incremental costs. Many banks realized this as a problem in the last decade when check volumes began to drop sharply, creating a "death spiral" in which the same fixed-cost base was spread over a smaller and smaller number of checks. With the advent of image clearing, however, banks were able to stop this process and reduce check processing costs.

- The payments industry is different from other processing industries in one very important aspect—the value of the money being transferred through the system. Providers who realize revenue related to the gross value of the payment transaction (the "amount") are more likely to have profitable businesses than those who realize revenue simply on a fee-per-transaction basis (a

---

Interchange

What is Interchange? Interchange is an element of payments system economics used by some open loop systems, particularly by card networks. Interchange is a transfer of value from one intermediary in a payments transaction to the other intermediary in that transaction. The payments system sets the interchange prices, but does not itself receive the value of interchange. Interchange creates an incentive for one "side" of the transaction to participate, by having the other "side" reimburse some of the costs incurred.

Payments Systems and Interchange: Some Have It, Some Don't In the U.S., the wire transfer, ACH, and checking open loop systems have traditionally operated without interchange—that is, there is no network-defined transfer of value between the "sending" and "receiving" banks to such transactions. Card network transactions do bear interchange. The sometimes dramatic difference in economics that results is fueling a number of different alternative payment schemes. The ACH system has recently approved a new processing model—"same day ACH"—which has an "interchange" component.

"click fee"). This type of "ad valorem" (percent of value) revenue may be direct (a fee calculated as a percentage of the amount of the transaction, or an interest rate applied to a loan balance) or indirect (the value of deposit balances held at a bank, or float).

- The economics of exception processing are critically important in payments systems. An exception item may occur simply because of a processing error (for example, a check shredded in a sorter). It may, in the case of a pull transaction, bounce. Or it may be the result of a customer inquiry or dispute. Typically, the cost of handling these exception items is much higher than the cost of handling a standard transaction. The efficiency with which a provider manages the exception process may significantly affect the overall economics of the product for that provider. In recent years, providers have been increasingly aggressive in pricing exception transactions to end parties. In some cases, the revenue from an exception transaction far exceeds the cost of the transaction, and contributes significantly to the profitability of the product. This is the case, for example, with bounced check fees, card over-limit fees, and, in most cases, overdraft fees.

Each bank sets its own price for services to its end party. Bank revenue can include fees and interest, as well as indirect components such as float.

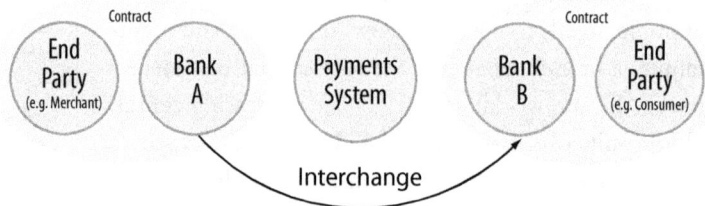

Figure 2-9: Economics of Open Loop Systems

In some systems, the network also defines a fee that flows from one bank to the other. This is called **interchange**.

Risk Management

All payments transactions are subject to risk. Some risks, notably that of fraud, have a very high public profile. But there are many types of risk, and all parties to a payments transaction bear some portion of the risk. The payment industry concentrates on three major form of risk:

- **Credit risk.** A credit card issuer bears obvious credit risk: the cardholder may simply fail to repay his or her loan balance. But there are other types of credit risk inherent in payments. Whenever a bank, for example, extends an overdraft rather than bouncing a pull payment (be it a debit card, check, or ACH debit), it incurs credit risk. Less obviously, a bank on the "send" side of a pull transaction (a card acquiring bank, or a check deposit bank) incurs credit risk because it is assuming financial responsibility for the actions of its customer.

- **Fraud risk.** As shown in the consumer and merchant example in the table below, there are many types of payments fraud risk, some specific to certain payments systems and others that are more general. Some payments systems, such as the card systems, have very high levels of system-defined fraud management. Others, such as checking and ACH, leave more of the fraud risk management to intermediaries and end parties.

> ### Risk, Float
>
> **Risk Pays**
> Whenever a provider—for example, a credit card issuer or a payments services provider—proactively assumes risk that another party would otherwise bear, it is apt to be well compensated. A provider that assumes risk but does not manage it well, or (worst case!) does not understand that it is assuming risk, is apt to have a short business life.
>
> **What is Float? (Part 1 of 2)**
> Float is the value earned from money held over a period of time. It is a benefit to a party that holds funds for a period of time before needing to pay them out. It is a cost to a party that needs to pay out funds prior to receiving them.

System	Consumer	Consumer's Bank	Network	Merchant's Bank	Merchant
Cash	Theft	Theft		Theft	Theft
Checking	Fraud	Fraud		Fraud, NSF	Fraud, NSF
Credit Card	Fraud	Fraud, Credit		Fraud	(Fraud)
Debit Card	Fraud	Fraud		Fraud	(Fraud)
ACH (Push)		Fraud			
ACH (Pull)	Fraud	Fraud		Fraud, NSF	Fraud, NSF
Wires		Fraud			

Notes: receiver's exposure is different in a card-not-present and non-EMV environment. Consumers have some protections against fraud with card network "zero liability" policies. Merchant's bank is exposed to merchant fraud.

Table 2-3: Payments Systems Fraud Exposures

- **Liquidity risk.** The risk that a party cannot fulfill its financial obligations to another party. In an open loop system, end parties have financial liability to their banks, and the banks have financial liability to the network. The network, in turn, has financial liability to the banks. The network's exposure is referred to as settlement risk. This stand-in function is the key to an open loop system: it means that a bank receiving money from another bank in the system need not worry about the liquidity of the sending bank. The network, however, does have to worry. If a network member fails (goes out of business) during the day while in a net debit position, the network (in most cases) must pay the obligation of that member to the other members. This is one reason why most open loop networks restrict membership to regulated financial institutions that meet certain capital standards and are subject to ongoing regulatory oversight.

Beyond these three primary forms of risk, there are many other secondary forms of risk:

• **Operational risk.** Occurs when one party to a transaction either fails to do what is expected or does something in error. A wide range of situations fall into this category: missed deadlines, incorrectly formatted files, machines that fail to start or operate correctly (e.g., check sorters jamming), etc. An operational error can have extremely serious financial consequences if, as a result, a party to the transaction ends up holding funds that it is obligated (by rules) to pass on to another party.

Each payments system has a combination of rules and working practices by which intermediaries in the system try to help each other recover from errors and avoid financial losses—but full recompense is not always possible. The role of processors and other third parties (meaning non-bank intermediaries in the value chain) is important to understanding operations risk. Often, a third party will provide "on behalf of" processing for a bank that bears formal legal responsibility, under the payments system rules, for a given task. If the third party errs in some way, the bank still remains liable. Because of this, many payments systems recognize the role of third parties and create rules—binding their direct members (the banks) to regulate and, at times, certify third-party involvement in the payments system.

• **Data security risk.** The risk that end party data held by a bank, processor, network, or other end party is exposed to actual or possible fraudulent use of the data. The actions taken by the card networks to create and enforce PCI-DSS (Payment Card Industry Data Security Standards) are an attempt to proactively manage this issue. More recently, the card industry has begun using issuer tokenization to further protect payment card credentials.

• **Reputation risk.** The risk that end parties lose faith in the integrity of the payments system. Recently in the United

States, the highly publicized loss of payment card data at merchants and processors has damaged the reputation of those companies resulting in some high-profile cases including the resignation of senior executives.

- **Regulatory risk.** Particularly in a time of change in payments practices, intermediaries, networks, and processors may be exposed to an indeterminate amount of risk due to unclear interpretation or application of private rules or government regulation. In addition, in most cases, innovation outpaces regulation—but regulation often catches up to address areas of potential consumer or systemic risks.

And finally, there is FX risk, or currency risk, associated with taking a position on a guaranteed transaction prior to the actual exchange rate being set or known.

Comparing Payments Systems

There are a number of factors to take into account when evaluating or comparing payments systems. As previously mentioned, the payments systems themselves compete with each other, particularly when there is a secular shift in payments behavior such as a move from cash to non-cash instruments. Payments systems providers look at this issue when considering whether to support new forms of payments. Payments systems users consider it when evaluating new payments forms.

- Open or closed loop?
- "Push" or "pull" payments?
- Net or gross settlement?
- Ownership—private vs. public; bank owned or not?
- Regulation—private rules and/or law/regulations?
- Batch or real-time processing?
- Economic model—at par?; is there interchange between participants?
- Which brand is used (and how)?
- Does the payment system define "products"?
- Do payment system rules determine:
  - If payment is guaranteed or not?
  - Timing of funding—before, at the time of, or after the transaction?

> ### *Thick or Thin?*
>
> Some payments networks are heavily resourced (i.e. have lots of money), enabling network-level investment in product definition, brand, risk management, and exception processing requirements. Visa, Mastercard, American Express and PayPal are all examples of what we call "thick model" networks. Other networks are thinly resourced, and manage only minimal interoperability issues, leaving functions such as product definition and brand to intermediaries. Check clearing houses, the ACH, and PIN debit networks are all examples of this "thin model."
>
> Many of these networks were originally bank-owned. Why would bank owners support a "thick model" in one instance and a "thin model" in another? We think it goes back to the reasons the network exists. In a "thick model," the network enables significant profits for its member banks. In a "thin model," the network exists to reduce costs (for example, in check processing), and so is operated as an efficient utility.
>
> In the U.S., the card industry started with the highly profitable credit card business, and one could argue that this is why the "thick model" was supported. The card networks have successfully carried this model over into the lower-margin debit card arena.

- How are exceptions handled?
- Fraud management procedures?
- Dispute handling—is it handled as part of the payment system?
- How are "on-us" transactions handled?

Over the years, we've had an opportunity to work with many payments systems entities and have developed a basic set of important economic factors that we believe drive the economics of payments systems:

- Risk pays—how do you assess and price for risk?
- "Ad valorem" fees are better than flat fees
- Cross-currency is lucrative
- Processing demands scale to be viable
- Businesses pay to be paid
- Banked consumers don't pay to pay; unbanked consumers generally do
- Exception processing is expensive
- Simplicity has economic value

Cross-Border Payments

Cross-border payments occur when an end party in one country pays an end party in another country. Let's look at how cross-border payments are made using open loop payments systems.

As background, remember that payments systems, by definition, operate on an in-country basis: only banks that are chartered or licensed to operate in a country may join a payments system in that country. Because of this, transferring money between countries often requires two separate transactions, one in the sending country and one in the receiving country. This is true even if the transaction is denominated in the same currency in both systems.

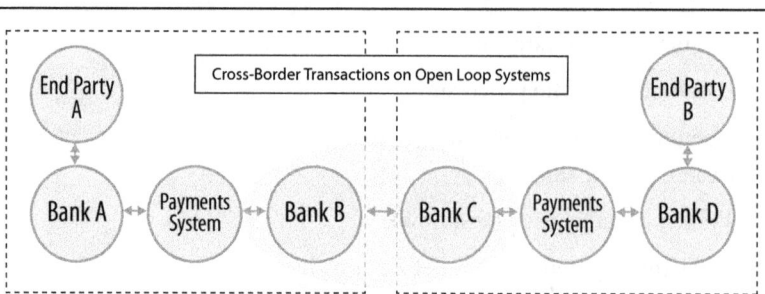

Figure 2-10: Cross-Border Payments

Each transaction must go through two payments systems, in two different countries. The intermediary banks (Banks B and C) settle their positions through correspondent accounts with each other, or with a third bank.

Of course, the two transactions must still be settled among the banks. This is done through a complex web of correspondent banking accounts that banks have with each other. These accounts may be housed in the sending country, the receiving country, or a third country. The global financial services messaging service SWIFT plays an important role in carrying instructions about these payments from one bank to another.

Effecting a single economic transaction in two separate payments systems (or more, in some cases) creates complexity and often confusion for the end parties. The systems may have different schedules, rules, and data formats. It is often difficult for the end party in one country (or even the bank in that country) to understand how a transaction will be treated in the receiving country. Hefty fees are not uncommon. The management of foreign exchange creates an additional level of complexity, and is often a source of considerable revenue to one or more parties to the transaction. The correspondent banking divisions of large banks manage such payments for their smaller bank customers.

Other Countries' Payments Systems

If you are interested in understanding another country's payments systems, a great place to start is at the website of the central bank of that country. Directly or indirectly, the central bank will have some regulatory control or oversight of the payments systems in its country.

Payments Systems Vary by Country, Not Region!

It is common to hear generalizations about regional payments systems or behaviors: "Everyone in Europe uses debit cards" or "Prepaid cards are common for Asian transit systems." The truth is that each country has its own story when it comes to payments systems. So don't trust the generalizations—examine individual country systems and patterns.

Although the types of payments systems available in each country are quite similar, the per capita usage of these systems varies considerably—for example, there's a dramatic difference in check usage between France (where checks have historically been popular) and Germany (where checks have been seldom used).

While this book is focused on United States payments systems, the principles discussed herein apply, generally speaking, to other countries as well.

Changing Payments Networks

Large-scale, open loop payments systems are highly efficient and scalable—the envy of many other industries that would like to achieve similar levels of smooth interoperability. (Think about the exchange of electronic medical records, for example!)

A downside of this structure is the inherent inertia in its systems. The fact that multiple remote parties can interact with each other easily, relying on a common body of standards, rules and liability frameworks, also means that it is very difficult to change these standards. Improvements or enhancements from one participant may have significant operational, technical, or economic ramifications that may not be immediately apparent at the time the change is proposed. Many proposed changes require simultaneous adjustments to technical standards, operations procedures, risk management procedures, pricing, and even the physical formatting of payments devices (checks, cards, terminals, etc.). Changing open loop payments systems can take years of work, first at a committee level (e.g., with representatives from the risk management groups at participating banks) and then at a senior management level within a network. Even once approved, a payments system change may not take effect for a year or more—giving participants time to prepare and implement changes.

Summary: U.S. Payments Systems

The various U.S. payments systems all move money, and they share many similar attributes. There are important differences among them, however. Understanding these differences is the key to appreciating the different utilities and economics of the systems. The table below gives a comparative overview of the core systems.

Payments System	Ownership & Regulation	Operations	Type	Interchange?	Risk Management
Cash	Virtual ownership; FRB and U.S. law regulation	No transaction processing; no settlement	Push	No	Recipient bears counterfeit risk
Check	Virtual ownership; FRB and U.S. law regulation; private rules	Batch processing; intrabank processing moving from paper to electronics; net settlement	Pull	No	Recipient bears fraud and NSF risk
ACH	Owned by banks; NACHA and FRB regulation	Batch processing; electronic; net settlement	Push or Pull	No (except for same day which bear interchange)	Recipient bears fraud and NSF risk ("pull" transactions)
Credit Card	Public or private ownership; non-bank; network rules and FRB regulation	Real-time authorization; batch clearing; net settlement	Pull	Yes	Recipient guaranteed good funds and protected from fraud (card-present transactions)
Debit Card	Public or private ownership; non-bank (except for some local/regional networks); network rules and FRB regulation	Real-time authorization; batch clearing; net settlement; PIN or signature cardholder verification	Pull	Yes	Recipient guaranteed good funds and protected from fraud (card-present transactions)
Wire Transfer	Bank ownership; FRB regulation	Real-time clearing and settlement	Push	No	Recipient guaranteed good funds and protected from fraud

Table 2-4: Summary: Core U.S. Payments Systems

Sources of Information on Payments Systems

There are many sources for information on the U.S. payments systems. Sources shown below are some good places to start. Further information is given at the end of the chapters on each of the core payments systems.

- PaymentsNews.com
- The Clearing House
- Federal Reserve Bank Payments Systems
- American Banker
- The Nilson Report
- Bank for International Settlements
- Country Central Banks

Core Systems: Checking

Type	"Pull" payments
Ownership	No single owner; check clearing houses owned by banks or private processors
Regulation	U.S. Law, network rules and Federal Reserve Bank regulation
Network Economics	Clears at par
Processing	Intrabank clearing by image or paper; batch
Risk Management	Managed by intermediaries and end parties

Table 3-1:
Overview—Checking

History and Background

The checking system in the United States is our oldest, and one of our most widely used open loop payments systems. The origins of the checking system as we know it today can be traced to medieval, and perhaps earlier, times—many economies developed some version of a document that allowed the transfer of funds from one bank to another. The word itself comes from the Arabic word şakk. There are many related payment-order documents, including bills of exchange, notes, drafts, and letters of credit, as well as specialized check forms such as counter checks, certified checks, and bank checks.

A check is considered a negotiable instrument. It instructs a bank to pay funds out of a checking account at a depository financial institution and provide those funds to the person or institution named on the check. As a negotiable instrument, checks can be transferred from one person to another. In the United States, checks are a service provided by banks and other financial institutions that have regulatory permissions to operate demand deposit accounts (DDAs), the more formal name for what we think of as checking accounts.

Today, the U.S. checking system is a highly automated means of transferring money from one end party to another. Despite the fact that a checking transaction begins with a piece of paper, almost all of today's check processing is electronic. This electronic processing, combined with very high transaction volumes, keeps the per-unit cost of checking relatively low.

A customer who presents, or deposits, a check to his or her bank creates a problem for that bank. The check is a claim on an account—usually at another bank. How does the consumer's bank collect the funds from the other bank? Historically, this process, known as clearing and settlement, happened bilaterally. The deposit bank would send a messenger to the other bank; the messenger would present the check and receive funds—perhaps in gold, cash, or banknotes—in return.

The development of the checking system from those early days in the United States can be divided into three significant phases, all marked by advances in the methodology of clearing and settlement.

Phase One: The Development of Clearing Houses

In the 18th and 19th centuries in the U.S., the number of banks—and the volume of checks written on them—grew, making the process of bilateral clearing and settlement more and more cumbersome. Messengers carried bags of checks to present to other banks; the cash or other instruments received in exchange were subject to theft.

In 1853, the first check clearing house was established in New York City. Banks joined the clearing house and brought, on every banking day, deposited checks drawn on other member banks. The clearing house facilitated an orderly exchange of checks among the banks and, importantly, calculated the daily net settlement for each bank. The banks then funded or drew from their settlement accounts. Soon similar clearing houses were established in other major cities, as were schemes for inter-city, regional, and national exchanges of checks between clearing houses.

The Federal Reserve Bank system, formed in the early 20th century, played an important role by requiring its member banks throughout the country to accept checks for deposit at par. This meant that the deposit bank would credit its customer with "one hundred cents on the dollar" rather than some lesser percentage. The Fed's requirement, coupled with the development of clearing houses across the country, transformed checking into a true national payments system.

Phase Two: Automation—MICR and Sorters

In the late 1950s and early 1960s, the introduction and widespread use of MICR (magnetic ink character recognition) characters enabled high-speed check processing. MICR characters, identifying the bank and account a check is drawn on, appear at the bottom of a check. The check amount is added after the check is written, usually by the bank of first deposit, in a process called encoding. Check sorters, used by banks on both sides of the process and by clearing houses and processors, read the MICR line and slot the individual checks into bins. They typically also capture an image of both sides of each check as it flows through the sorter.

Other developments further enabled national-scale automated check processing. The use by depository financial institutions of a uniform bank numbering scheme—the transit routing number assigned by the American Banking Association— was an important element. The gradual dissolution of laws prohibiting interstate banking resulted in a number of large national and regional banks concentrating on a broader definition of "on-us": for the first time, many banks found themselves members of multiple clearing houses. The need for long and cumbersome chains of correspondent banks for processing out-of-region checks was reduced by the advent of large-scale air transportation services. Processors serving smaller banks developed "on-we" check-clearing capabilities that mimicked, to some extent, the multi-state check processing capabilities of national banks.

Phase Three: Imaging

While MICR and check sorting equipment automated the exchange of checks, banks still had to manage and store paper checks. This was a particular burden on the check writer's bank, which had to keep each physical check, often returning it to its writer with the monthly statement. Others in the chain, including the deposit bank, intermediary banks, and processors, might need to see the paper check to resolve a dispute or inquiry, resulting in a tedious and costly exercise. When imaging technology began to mature in the late 1980s and 1990s, banks saw an opportunity to reduce the internal costs of storing checks and retrieving them for use in inquiries. Banks began to add cameras onto their check sorters, capturing an image of each document as it went through the machine.

> ### *What If?*
>
> If the checking system had gone in another direction, adopting instead a discounted (not par) clearing and settlement model, it might have looked a lot like our interchange-based card payments system. A merchant receiving a check for $100 might deposit the check to its bank, which would credit the merchant's account for $98. The bank would then present the check to the consumer's bank, receiving $98 in credit. The consumer's bank would debit its customer's account for $100, keeping the remaining $2 as profit on the transaction.
>
> Some industry observers have suggested the Fed impose a similar "at par" model on debit card transactions, which are analogous to checks, with the exception of the "good funds" and fraud guarantees provided by cards. The Fed was not persuaded to do so, resulting in increased lobbying efforts to secure legislation along those lines. The passage of the Durbin Amendment as part of the Dodd-Frank Act passed by Congress in 2008 was likely influenced by these efforts.

Banks spent over a decade investing in and learning to use image technology, primarily for archiving purposes. Using images for clearing—exchanging images rather than paper—was a logical extension. Bankers worked together during this time, in a variety of groups, to explore "electronic checking" and "check truncation." Some large banks did exchange images. Others exchanged MICR line data files for posting, with physical checks following, using private, multi-party agreements to do so. In either case, the underlying law still required that presentment to the check writer's bank be made with the original paper check. This greatly hampered efforts to clear by image, as banks anywhere along the line could need access to the original paper check in the event of a dispute, inquiry, or error.

The Check Clearing for the 21st Century Act (Check 21), which took effect in October 2004, solved this problem. Check 21 was proposed and sponsored by the Federal Reserve Bank, who wanted the industry to move towards electronic clearing, but did not want to mandate it.

Rather than mandating image clearing, the Check 21 law simply states that a printed copy of the original check (a "substitute check" or "image replacement document"—IRD) is the legal equivalent of the original paper check.

A bank may still refuse to accept images—but it must accept a printed copy of the image. Practically, this has meant that a bank of deposit, physically far removed from the check writer's bank, can send an image (usually through a clearing house) to a printer near the check writer's bank; the printout is presented on behalf of the deposit bank.

Today in the U.S., the check payment system is almost entirely electronic—as imaging has proven to be an important advance that improves check collection speed, reduces risk, and lowers operational costs.

> ### *Grounded Planes*
>
> The events of September 11, 2001, are often cited as the reason for the Fed's actions in championing the Check 21 law. When planes didn't fly, and checks didn't move—for days after the attacks—the float at the Federal Reserve Bank (which technically acts as a correspondent bank in check processing: checks presented to the Fed for clearing are deposited into presenting bank's account at a Federal Reserve Bank) mounted to alarming levels, as the Fed was not able to onwardly present the checks to paying banks. In fact, the Fed had been actively working on promoting a Check 21 type of law for some time: 9/11 served as an impetus to move this forward.

Roles and the Value Chain

The checking payments system, at its most basic, has three parties involved: the check writer, the recipient of the check, and the bank into which the check is deposited. If, as is most typical, the check writer and recipient are using different banks, there are four parties. The checking value chain is illustrated below:

In the checking system, it is the job of the bank of first deposit (also known as the presenting bank) to get the check to the check writer's bank (also known as the paying bank). The presenting bank will be credited by the paying bank only upon presentment of the item.

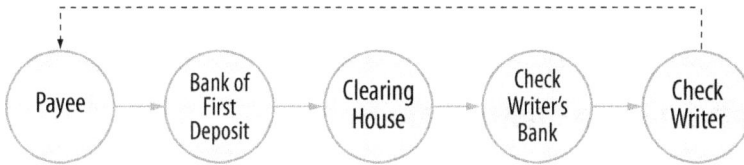

Payee → Bank of First Deposit → Clearing House → Check Writer's Bank → Check Writer

The presenting bank may present the item to the paying bank however it likes; today, it is almost always by image.

Figure 3-1:
The Checking
Value Chain

The check writer's bank offers its customer—whether a consumer, business, nonprofit, or government entity—a demand deposit account with checking as a feature. The check writer's bank provides the customer either with blank check stock or with the details (transit routing number and account number) to put on check stock that the customer provides or creates.

The check writer writes the check, specifying the payee, the date, and the dollar amount of the check. Writing may be manual, as with a consumer, or accomplished via an automated printing process, as with large corporations.

> **Checking: Our Newest Electronic Payment System**
>
> The results of Check 21 have been dramatic. Most banks began serious implementation of check image clearing in 2007. By early 2010, the Fed announced that 99% of checks clearing through the Fed were being processed electronically.

The check writer then delivers the check to the recipient. The recipient deposits the check to a bank where the recipient has a demand deposit account. (Alternatively, the recipient may endorse the check and give it to a non-bank intermediary, which then assumes the role of recipient of the check.)

The deposit bank credits the customer's account and makes the deposit available for use by their customer (such as withdrawing cash) according to its funds availability policy. The deposit bank's availability policy is constrained by Federal Reserve Bank Regulation CC, which dictates the minimum availability for checks of various kinds. Many banks, however, provide more generous availability terms than are required by regulation; this is a source of competition among banks, particularly for small-business checking accounts.

The complexity of the checking payments system is revealed at this point in the chain, when the recipient's bank, or bank of first deposit, must decide how to clear the check—that is, how to get the check to the check writer's bank.

The bank of first deposit is under no legal or regulatory constraint to clear the check in any particular way—it is free to deliver the check to the paying bank through a clearing house, through a bilateral arrangement with that bank, by depositing the check with a correspondent bank (which then becomes the "bank of second deposit"), or by turning the check over to a processor that makes the clearing decision.

The Pre-Image Clearing Environment

The Deposit Bank

A deposit bank, historically, would make these decisions by evaluating questions such as the dollar value of the check, the time of day of the deposit, distance to the paying bank, and commercial flight schedules. These factors were important because the paying bank's obligation to fund the presentment occurred upon physical presentment of the check. The deposit bank must assess the tradeoff between getting funds faster (by delivering a check quickly) and managing delivery costs (by using a low-cost delivery mechanism). The deposit bank's presentment decision policies were input to the check sorter, which then slotted check items into bins for clearing by various methods, and to various paying banks.

The Great Value of the Checking System?

A little-noticed feature of checking is the fact that the check writer does not need to know, transmit, or store any information about the recipient's bank or bank account number. One could think of this as built-in PCI-DSS compliance! Of course, the check writer is sending his own account data (visible on the check), which creates another type of potential fraud exposure.

The Clearing House

Most checks in the pre-imaging environment were cleared through a clearing house. A clearing house receives checks from the deposit bank, accompanied by a cash letter—basically, a deposit slip showing how many checks are being presented and for what value. Most typically, the checks brought to the clearing house were already pre-sorted into bags or bundles for each paying bank. The checks were exchanged, and the clearing house then calculated net settlement totals for the banks involved in the clearing house. A clearing house may run this settlement process itself, or may contract it out to the Federal Reserve Bank (which runs a settlement service) or other settlement provider.

Clearing Complexities

U.C.C. 4: "A collecting bank shall send items by a reasonably prompt method, taking into consideration relevant instructions, the nature of the item, the number of those items on hand, the cost of collection involved, and the method generally used by it or others to present those items."

The Paying Bank

The paying bank receives checks from the clearing house and again runs them through a sorter, creating a file of transaction detail that is used to post transactions to check writers' accounts. Historically, these postings were done during the bank's nightly batch run of the DDA system. If, after the run, an account did not have sufficient funds to pay a check posted to the account, the paying bank could either keep the transaction and extend an overdraft loan to the customer, or reject the transaction and "bounce" it back to the presenting bank. This decision, of course, was usually automated, dictated by policies programmed into the bank's DDA system. If the bank keeps the check, and sustains the overdraft, the overdraft becomes a loan subject to the lending policies of the institution.

Rendezvous

In some cities decades ago, a "check clearing house" was little more than a place—maybe even a parking lot—where banks agreed to meet to exchange bags of checks!

Blind Posting

Both checks and ACH debit (check-like) transactions are posted to the customer's account on what can be thought of as a "blind" basis. By this, we mean that the consumer's bank does not check, prior to the posting, whether or not there are sufficient funds in the account. There is no authorization process for checks that is equivalent to that used with credit or debit cards.

Image Clearing

The Deposit Bank

In an image-processing environment, the deposit bank will typically image all checks deposited payable by another bank. Where a check image is "captured" varies by bank. Highly automated banks capture most items at the point of deposit—in the ATM or at the branch teller's window. Other banks capture deposits in back-office processing centers, or deliver the paper items to a processor that handles the capture for them. The bank (or its processor) then determines whether a given item is presented under some form of bilateral arrangement with the paying bank, through some form of clearing house, or by conversion to ACH. If converted to ACH, the items must conform with NACHA rules for that transaction type.

What happens next depends very much on the deposit bank in question. It is easier to think in terms of the functions that need to occur, rather than what entities perform them. The deposit bank must:

- Deliver the images to the paying bank—either directly or through a service or processor
- Ensure that IRDs (image replacement documents) are printed out and delivered to paying banks that do not want to receive images
- Settle with the paying bank

A processor or a clearing house may handle all or some of these tasks.

Image Clearing—The Future

There are a number of scenarios under discussion, and in some cases in practice, within the industry. Immediate, dynamic presentation of a check image from an ATM (used to make a deposit) to a paying bank is one possibility. If the paying bank adopts real-time posting (rather than waiting to post during a nightly batch run), then the deposit bank would know immediately if a check bounces. Another possibility is that the image itself not be directly presented to the paying bank, but rather held in an archive accessible by either bank. In this case, the deposit bank would simply send the MICR information to the paying bank, along with the archive address, and the paying bank would post the item from this file.

Ownership and Regulation

Ownership

No single entity owns the checking payments system. Each bank chooses how to support checking, for both checks written on its demand deposit accounts and checks deposited into its accounts. Banks usually belong to one or more check clearing houses—traditionally, bank-owned cooperatives operating on a nonprofit basis. Today, some clearing houses continue to be owned by banks, while others are owned by for-profit companies. Large processors that offer check processing to banks are similar in some functions to clearing houses.

The Image of Image Clearing

Moving intrabank processing of check payments from paper to electronic makes a payments system that was already highly efficient even more so. The time taken to clear items has shortened dramatically, and checks, at times, now clear faster than ACH or cards. Perhaps most significant, the costs of transporting checks around the country have been largely eliminated. A check can now be thought of as an up-front paper order to pay—a kind of one-time payment card.

Regulation

The regulatory framework for checking is U.S. law—specifically, the Uniform Commercial Code. Article 3 and Article 4 of the U.C.C. specifies provisions around bank deposits and collections and the liability of various parties in a checking transaction. When the U.C.C. was published in the early 1950s, and adopted by each of the 50 states, it helped to create a uniform legal framework for commercial transactions in general—and checking specifically—and reduced some legal complexities of the system. The 2004 Check 21 law was the next major U.S. law to affect checking. As previously described, Check 21 makes a substitute check (a printed copy of an image of an original check called an image replacement document) the legal equivalent of the original.

The Federal Reserve Bank, in its role as regulator, issues regulations that implement checking law. Key Fed regulations for checking include Regulations J and CC, which together specify provisions around check availability and other aspects of check clearing. If a deposit bank is using the Federal Reserve Bank's payments services to clear checks, they are subject to the Fed's Operating Circular 3.

Check clearing houses have system rules that bind participating banks, governing presentment times, conventions for batching and cash letters, and other operational issues. Clearing house rules are not the equivalent in scope of payments system rules in card and ACH payments—they do not cover requirements for check products offered by banks to their customers. Check and image processing companies also have operations rules that are similar in scope.

ECCHO (Electronic Check Clearing House Organization) is a nonprofit bank cooperative (technically, a mutual benefit clearing house) that has written rules for image exchange. Banks exchanging images bilaterally, or image clearing houses, may elect to subscribe to these rules; however, these rules only apply to items exchanged among ECCHO members.

Check Use, Volumes, and Trends

Since the checking payments system is so large and decentralized, it is difficult to pinpoint volumes with any certainty. The Federal Reserve Bank periodically commissions surveys of check volumes at selected banks; these are used to project national volumes. Some such surveys look at individual items in order to determine estimates of who the payers are, who the payees are, and what the purpose of the check is.

Check volumes are very large but are declining rapidly in some segments. Data from recent Federal Reserve Payments Studies show an overall sharp decline—but particularly sharp drops in certain domains, such as point of sale (POS) payments and bill payment—a shown in the table below.

Type of Check	2001	2006	2009	2012	% Change
Business to business	9.1	8.3	7.9	5.9	-35%
Business to consumer	8.9	5.6	5.2	3.1	-65%
Consumer to business	27.9	17.0	12.3	9.6	-66%
Consumer to consumer	5.6	2.2	2.4	2.4	-54%

Source: 2013 Federal Reserve Payments Study

Table 3-2: Checks Written (count in billions)

Some checks that are written, however, are not paid as checks, but are rather converted to ACH (see Chapter 4).

Check Regulation in Transition

It is important to note that with the transition from paper-based checks to image-based checks, the laws and regulations that apply to paper checks do not apply by default to check image exchanges. This creates risk of uncertainty for all parties when disputes arise. Image exchange agreements between all the parties are the means used to address this risk.

Check Economics

The economics of the U.S. checking system can be understood by first looking at check-based products sold to end parties, then at the underlying processing and clearing infrastructure that supports these products. Banks, in particular, offset costs from check-processing platforms with revenues from a number of different check products. Processing costs are changing at a dizzying rate, as the absolute volume of checks decline and, more significantly, the means of check clearing changes from paper to electronic.

Check Products

Checking Accounts—Consumers and Small Businesses

Banks offer consumers and small businesses check writing and deposit capabilities as part of bundled "checking account" products. Writing or depositing individual checks is seldom separately priced. Banks see check writing, in particular, as an essential element of a package that brings deposits to the bank. Banks do charge NSF (non-sufficient funds) fees for checks written on insufficient funds that the bank chooses not to return; historically, this has been a significant source of bank revenue. Small business checking accounts work the same way (and, in fact, typically share the same delivery platform), but often have caps on the number of checks that can be written in a given month, with transaction fees charged if the volume is exceeded. For both consumers and small businesses, banks see checking as a necessary component in an account package that brings in revenue from the value of interest income earned on the balance in the account, debit card interchange, and fees.

Checking Accounts—Large Enterprises

Large enterprises write many checks for payroll, benefits, and vendor payments. Banks offer checking accounts with transaction fee schedules for these enterprises. The enterprise may use the value of their "compensating balances" in their accounts to completely or partially offset the fees (called "account analysis"). A specialized checking account, called a controlled disbursement account, is used to help the enterprise understand and control the timing of checks presented for payment against the account. This information and control is important for a company wanting to optimize its use of cash, allowing better borrowing and investment decisions to be made. Positive pay fraud control (a check is paid by the bank only if it matches a check number and amount on a file provided to the bank by the enterprise) and automated account reconcilement are typical supporting services on these accounts.

Lockbox Services—Enterprises

Both banks and non-banks offer specialty products to serve enterprises that receive checks from consumers or other businesses.

Retail lockbox services are designed to handle large volumes of checks from consumers (to a utility or insurance company, for example). A retail lockbox provider controls a post office box to which consumer checks are directed. The provider picks up envelopes from the post office several times a day, opens the envelopes, encodes the checks, sends them into clearing, scans the remittance advice (which the consumer has put into the envelope with the check), and creates a file of payments received for the enterprise customer to use in updating its billing files. This is a highly automated and historically low-margin business. The value proposition to the enterprise customer is accelerated collection of funds and automated data capture. Pricing is on a per-transaction basis, with additional charges for data feeds, etc.

Wholesale lockbox services are similar, but focus on high-value checks received from business customers. The incoming remittance advices are each different (the format is determined by the paying customer's check-printing system) and the process of capturing data from them is less automated and more expensive. The value of wholesale lockbox traditionally is heavily dependent on faster clearing of high-value checks—automated data capture is secondary.

Image clearing and remote deposit check capture are significantly changing the dynamics of this business. Many wholesale lockbox providers now handle inbound ACH payments and inbound checks, creating a single point of information about bank deposits and remittance data feeds. Pricing is on a per-transaction and often per-keystroke-entered basis, with additional charges for data feeds.

Remote Deposit Capture

Remote deposit capture (RDC) products are offered by banks to consumers and enterprises of all sizes. With the advent of mobile smartphone technologies that include cameras for capturing check images, the popularity of RDC has skyrocketed—as it helps avoid a trip to the local ATM or bank branch to make a deposit!

This service, shown below, allows the payee to scan and electronically deposit a check it receives.

Remote deposit capture is a product offered to a payee, most typically a small or medium-sized merchant or other business. The payee captures an image of the check and electronically "deposits" it —either to the payee's bank or to a third-party processor, which then deposits it.

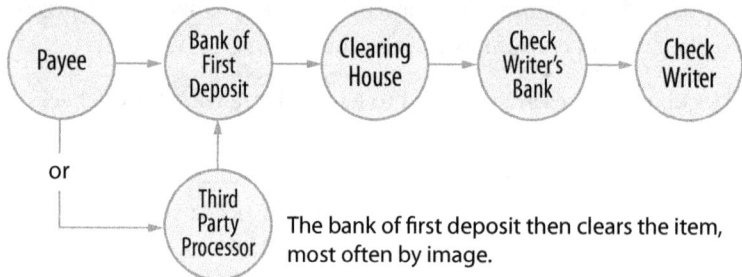

The bank of first deposit then clears the item, most often by image.

Figure 3-2: Remote Deposit Capture

The RDC provider assumes the risk that the enterprise has scanned a valid paper check. If the provider is a non-bank, the image is deposited in a bank. In either case, the bank can then submit it for clearing as an image or, at its option, convert it to a substitute check and clear it as paper. The value proposition to the enterprise is the time and costs saved by not physically depositing the check. Providers are becoming more flexible regarding the scanning devices supported for the service. Remote deposit capture is typically priced on a flat per-transaction basis or may simply be bundled into the overall cost for the account.

Retail Merchant Check Deposit Services

Large retail merchants have historically received high volumes of checks in payment for purchases. Unlike billers, merchants must make an acceptance decision at the point of payment. Many retailers use automated systems to decide whether or not to accept a check, based on reading the MICR line at an ECR (electronic cash register) or a terminal with check reading capabilities. The decisioning system may simply use data from the retailer's internal system (a file of known bad-check writers, for example), or may access external databases. A retailer may opt to have the check verified (determining if the account is real and in good standing), or even guaranteed, by service providers offering these options.

Most large retailer systems encode checks as received (put the dollar amount on the MICR line) to avoid bank charges for doing so. The retailer pays a per-transaction deposit fee to the bank or the non-bank party accepting the transaction. If the retailer is using a check guarantee service, the provider charges a fixed fee plus a percent of value charge; this makes the economics of the transaction similar to those of credit card acceptance.

Retail merchants need to determine if checks received will be converted to ACH and, if so, whether they will be converted at the cash register (POP, or Point of Purchase format), or in the back office (BOC, or Back Office Conversion format), converted to image (remote deposit capture), or deposited as paper. If converting to ACH, NACHA rules place restrictions on what types of checks may be converted. Some retailers do this in house. Others turn the checks over to a service provider that makes the decisions, and processes and deposits transactions, on their behalf.

Increasingly, as debit cards have grown in popularity, many retail merchants have decided to stop accepting checks altogether. Of course, this limitation on check acceptance helps fuel even further debit card usage by consumers.

Other Check Products—Consumers

Consumers buy (or are given) blank checkbooks from either their banks or third-party check printers—companies that also supply banks with check stock.

Unbanked consumers use check equivalents offered by non-banks. Check cashing services allow consumers to cash checks by endorsing the check over to the service. Money orders are sold by stores, the post office, and other retail service providers.

There are also a number of specialty consumer checking products, including traveler's checks, certified checks, cashier's checks, and bank checks.

Other Check Products—Enterprises

Many small businesses write checks using accounting software packages (for example, QuickBooks); the software companies and other providers supply check stock to work with these packages.

Some large enterprises print checks in house, using a check printer that receives its data feed from the enterprise's accounts payable and/or payroll system. Others outsource the process to check printing services. This is particularly common for payroll applications, with the service managing multiple aspects of payroll (tax calculations, retirement contributions, etc.). Such services also manage the enterprise's ACH payroll payments.

Check Clearing and Infrastructure Economics

Banks, clearing houses, and processors all participate in the economic value chain for check clearing. Banks generally have separate operational areas to handle check deposit processing and "in-clearing," the process of receiving checks presented to the bank for payment. Either or both of these areas may be outsourced to a processor.

The bank or processor has operational expenses associated with accepting or delivering paper checks; operating check sorters; imaging and archiving checks; running and maintaining the applications that apply bank policy to individual items to determine check posting times, funds availability, and overdrafts; and managing the reconcilement of settlement accounts. Clearing houses have expenses associated with determining settlement totals, and managing the settlement process.

> **Bundling Check and Card Acceptance**
>
> Many card acquirers and their ISOs bundle check acceptance with card acceptance, particularly for small and mid-sized businesses. Just as a card acquirer will handle a card payment for a retailer, then deposit the proceeds into the bank account specified by that retailer, so will it handle a check—usually through remote deposit capture and/or ACH conversion.

Processors and clearing houses charge transaction fees to banks that use their services. Many banks provide correspondent services to smaller banks: the bigger bank may act as a processor and handle check processing, again on a transaction-fee basis, but with an account analysis factor (giving the smaller bank credit for the value of balances held at its bank).

In general, banks and processors have significant expenses associated with bounced checks and exception items; these costs can greatly exceed the cost of "normal" items. Banks use the expression "Day 2 Processing" to refer to all activities (returns, adjustments, statement rendering, research, etc.) resulting after acceptance or refusal of an item by the paying bank.

A final, important element of check economics—for all parties—is the cost of fraud, and of fraud (and other risk) management.

Risk Management

Check fraud has a long and colorful history. It falls into many categories, including forged checks; forged signatures on legitimate checks; altered amounts, dates, or payees; fraudulent endorsement; and scheme frauds such as check kiting. Writing a check on insufficient funds in an account (called NSF), while technically fraud, is generally seen as a separate category of risk exposure as the check writer may or may not be aware of the insufficient fund situation.

Non-Sufficient Funds (NSF) Risk

The payee accepting a check is exposed to the risk of the check "bouncing." If the check writer's bank pays the check on insufficient funds, the risk of collecting from the consumer moves to the bank (as does the revenue from an NSF fee to the consumer!). When a bounced check is returned, the depository bank debits its customer's account; if that customer has since drained the funds from the account, that bank is at risk. Payees (or their banks) may re-present a bounced check for payment, either as paper, by image, or via an ACH transaction. As discussed above, payees, particularly retailers, may use internal or external databases or services to help manage this risk. Payees may also choose to purchase check verification or guarantee services.

Retail merchants, billers, and enterprises are the most exposed to NSF risk. Industry estimates of annual losses are in the range of $10 billion, though no precise figures are known. Bank losses to NSF are not disclosed, but are much smaller. Banks, in general, find these losses acceptable given the very lucrative NSF fee revenue collected from their consumers.

Check Fraud

If a check is forged on a valid account, or a valid check is altered, and a payee accepts this and deposits it, someone is going to lose money on the fraud. The check writer's bank has a legal obligation to pay an item when it is "properly payable"; the check writer, like the other parties, has a responsibility to exercise "ordinary care." Provisions in the U.C.C. as well as a significant amount of case law result in major losses due to fraud being allocated by the courts—or by arbitration—to various parties to the transaction. Determining exposure is complex, particularly given the transition to imaging and subsequent regulatory complications. Practically speaking, merchants (and billers) end up with quite a bit of exposure, as do check writing corporations. Merchant losses due to bounced checks are believed to be significantly higher than from other types of check fraud. In the U.S., bank exposure to check fraud is generally believed to be less than $1 billion annually.

Counterfeit checks (including counterfeit cashier's checks) are drawn on non-existent accounts. Such checks become the responsibility of the depository

> ### What is Float? (Part 2 of 2)
>
> Float is an integral part of the economics of the checking system, and also one of the most misunderstood terms in the business! This is partly because the term is used in multiple ways. In the abstract, float refers to a gap in the availability of funds transferred between two parties.
>
> Sometimes this is concrete: "Federal Reserve float" occurs when the Fed, acting as a check clearing house, credits a deposit bank for funds received, prior to collecting from the paying bank. (Historically, the Fed has done this as a way to manage, on behalf of the presenting bank, uncertainties in check collection.)
>
> Often float is more a matter of perception: "disbursement float" is a term used to describe the gap between when a corporation mails a check (and presumably discharges its obligation to a vendor) and the time that the check is actually presented to its bank for payment.
>
> Float is often discussed in relative terms: if a bank has been collecting deposited checks on an average of 1.5 days after receipt, and it reduces that to an average of 1.25 days, it has improved float. If a bank makes good funds available to a depositing customer prior to receiving payment on the check in question, it is incurring a float expense—which may be theoretical, rather than actual, if the customer in question leaves the balances in the account.
>
> Confused? Here's one thing to remember about float. Image clearing, and related products and concepts (ACH check conversion, remote deposit capture), are greatly reducing the amount—and importance—of float in the U.S. checking system.

bank, which then attempts to reclaim funds from the depositing customer's account.

Technology and Check Fraud

Today's high-resolution scanners and printers have made it much easier to forge checks on legitimate accounts. Also, the ability to see images of paid checks during an online banking session is causing bankers anxiety, as phished credentials could allow fraudsters to see a "perfect image" of a check, providing a template for forgery. Despite these issues, banks have apparently been able to keep the overall level of check forgery under control.

Risk Management Products

To help minimize fraud, retailers buy check verification and guarantee products, as discussed above, as well as access to external databases. Banks buy similar products to guide the decision to accept a check for deposit and cashing; the banking industry collaborates on a database, administered by Early Warning Services, that provides this data. Bank processors provide software that helps identify fraudulent transactions by examining patterns of transactions within and across accounts. (Similar software is used to detect transactions that violate money-laundering regulation.) Banks and retailers use a wide range of products and services to detect check forgeries, identify fraudulent signatures, etc.

Fed Actions

The Fed took two parallel actions to encourage the industry to move to image clearing. It sponsored and championed the law that was eventually passed as "Check 21." But it also announced a series of decisions to shut down local check processing (clearing house) facilities used by banks throughout the country. This meant that banks had to send paper checks farther, at greater expense—making them more eager to implement image clearing.

Major Providers

The Federal Reserve Bank

The Federal Reserve Board and the Federal Reserve Banks (together, "the Fed") have a unique position in the checking industry. "The Fed" plays three roles:

- As a payments industry regulator, it writes the rules that govern practices by banks and other parties across multiple payments systems.

- As a provider of payments services, it operates the largest check and check image clearing houses in the country. (It also operates one of the two ACH switches and one of the two wire transfer systems (Fedwire), and is the sole provider of cash and currency to banks.) The Fed sells these services only to banks.

- As the manager of the National Settlement Service, it provides settlement services to multiple private sector clearing houses, both paper and electronic.

The Clearing House

The Clearing House, a bank-owned payments company, is a quiet power-house in the banking industry. Originally the New York Clearing House (for check clearing), established in 1853, it grew through a series of mergers with other clearing houses and payments companies, and through establishing new payments services to serve its member banks. Today it is owned by twenty-four large banks (both U.S. banks and the U.S. branches of international banks). It is a major competitor to the Fed in providing payments services to banks—offering check and image clearing, ACH processing (it's the one other ACH operator in the country), and, through CHIPS, wire transfer processing.

Summary: Checking

Checking, long the dominant non-cash payments system in the U.S., is in decline. But radical changes in check clearing practices have transformed the economics of the system.

Key Trends in Checking

- Check volumes are still large, but are dropping overall, and most sharply in POS and bill payment domains.

- Image clearing and check-to-ACH conversion have drastically changed bank clearing practices and the unit cost of handling checks.

- Remote image capture by ATMs, branches, and end parties is lowering the cost of check acceptance, and reducing float and risk.

- Working groups are looking at "fully electronic checks" (one possible term—EPO, or electronic payment order)—an instrument that begins as a check image.

Sources of Information—Checking

- PaymentsNews.com
- ECCHO
- The Clearing House
- The Federal Reserve Bank Retail Payments Office
- Individual Federal Reserve Banks
- Financial Services Technology Consortium
- Bank Administration Institute (BAI)

Core Systems: ACH

Type	"Push" and "pull" payments
Ownership	Owned by banks
Regulation	NACHA rules and Federal Reserve Bank regulation
Network Economics	Clears at par except for "same day"
Processing	Electronic, batch
Risk Management	Left to intermediaries and end parties

Table 4-1: ACH Overview

History and Background

The ACH, or Automated Clearing House, is one of the largest payments networks in the United States. It is a bank-owned utility used for many different types of consumer and enterprise applications. The non-profit association, NACHA—formerly the National Automated Clearing House Association, but now NACHA: The Electronic Payments Association—serves as the trustee of the ACH network and manages the regulatory and rule making processes, which then define the NACHA Operating Rules.

The ACH system was started in the 1970s by bankers working in check processing automation. With the introduction of check readers/sorters, it became obvious that all that was required to post transactions to customer accounts was the MICR data. "Why not," these bankers asked, "simply exchange MICR data directly, rather than exchanging checks and then extracting the MICR data?" Note that this was not an early attempt at check truncation or check image clearing—it focused instead on having the electronic transaction replace the paper transaction entirely.

Note: To really understand the ACH system, first read Chapter 3, Checking. The ACH was created by many of the same people who ran checking operations in banks.

Bankers focused, in the early days of ACH, on high-volume, low-risk, repetitive transactions—particularly payroll checks, social security benefit checks, and insurance premium payments.

The result is that the ACH, more than any other payments network in the United States, is wired in to every demand deposit account in the country. An enterprise wishing to make or collect a payment using one of the ACH transaction types can do so, and safely plan on being able to reach every banked consumer and enterprise in the country. In addition, consumers holding general purpose reloadable (GPR) prepaid cards (see Chapter 5) can have funds deposited into those card accounts by the ACH.

Cracking the Chicken and the Egg Problem

The fledgling ACH network was formed in the mid-1970s. It was designed to keep costs low for participating banks. In most parts of the country, local ACH associations were formed by bankers participating in each area's check clearing house. But participation was still optional and, in the early days, the network faced the same "chicken and egg" problem faced by all new payments networks. For the ACH, the question was, "How do we get consumers to sign up for ACH (say, for direct deposit of pay checks) if most banks don't participate? And how do we get banks to participate if we don't have consumers asking to be paid this way?" The answer, in this case, was the government. The U.S. government offered to pay Social Security benefits via ACH. It asked banks, in effect, "Do you have any customers who receive social security benefits?" The answer, of course, was yes—and over a period of 15 years virtually all "depository financial institutions," including thrifts, savings and loans, and credit unions, joined the ACH network.

Roles and the Value Chain

As background to this section, it is important to understand that the ACH is the only payments system in the U.S. that handles both push and pull payments transactions:

- A "push" transaction (referred to as an ACH Credit) is initiated by the payer of funds, and sends money to the receiving party.

- A "pull" transaction (referred to as an ACH Debit) is initiated by the receiver of funds, and pulls money from the paying party.

The basic roles, and the core value chain, are the same for both "push" and "pull" payments—as shown below—though, as we will see, the risks and economics are quite different for each type.

In the ACH system, an **originator** delivers transactions to its bank. Each bank in the system chooses an operator. The operator sorts and forwards the transactions to receiving banks or other operators.

The ACH Value Chain

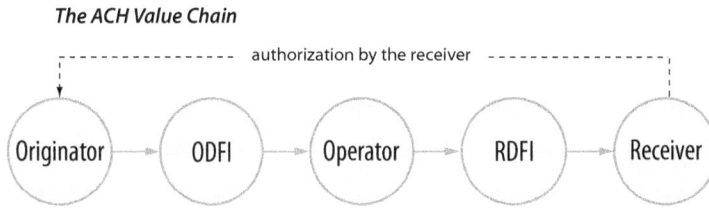

The flow is exactly the same for both push and pull transactions. The originator is responsible for obtaining the receiver's authorization for the transaction. The ODFI is liable to the network for the actions of its originator clients.

Figure 4-1: The ACH Value Chain

An ACH transaction is entered into the ACH payments system by an originator, most typically an enterprise. The originator delivers the transaction to its bank, called the ODFI, or originating depository financial institution. The ODFI credits or debits its customer's account (depending whether the transaction is "pull" or "push") and forwards the transaction to its chosen ACH operator. The operator performs a switch role, passing the transactions on to the RDFI, or receiving depository financial institution. (If the ODFI and the RDFI use different ACH operators—there are only two in the U.S.—the first operator switches the transaction to the second operator.) The RDFI then debits or credits the account of its customer (the recipient), again depending on whether the transaction is "pull" or "push".

ACH Settlement

Today, ACH operators calculate net settlement totals for their banks on a daily basis. These totals are submitted to the Fed, which manages the actual settlement process using its National Settlement Service. Practically speaking, this results in "zero float" among the banks and their clients—although some banks may manage the timing of debits or credits to client accounts in order to accommodate risk policies.

ACH "Direct Sends"

As with checking, it is possible for two banks (or groups of banks) to exchange transactions bilaterally rather than using one of the ACH operators. Although this does occur, the extreme low cost and efficiency of the operators discourages banks from doing this.

Ownership and Regulation

The ACH is owned, in effect, by the banks (depository financial institutions) that belong to it. NACHA is a nonprofit association that oversees the network. Depository financial institutions (referred to here as "banks") belong to NACHA either directly or through a local or regional payments association. The NACHA bylaws govern how voting power is allocated among the bank and payments association members.

NACHA's Role

NACHA's primary role is rule making, discussed below. Unlike the card networks, NACHA is not involved in processing. Transaction switching among the intermediary banks is done by an ACH operator. (Currently, there are two operators—the Federal Reserve Bank and Electronic Payments Network (EPN), owned by The Clearing House.)

A Question of Brand?

It will be interesting to observe how the brand question plays out in the eCommerce domain. Today, we see third-party brands appearing alongside the card brands on checkout pages, but if a merchant accepts ACH "eChecks," they are apt to put a descriptor such as "pay with your bank account."

NACHA is actively involved with its member institutions, and their corporate clients, in developing and testing product enhancements and new products. It does not, however, operate on the same scale as the card networks. It has a significantly lower budget than the networks, and is therefore limited in developing new products for distribution through member banks.

NACHA does not play a role in brand creation or communication. In this way, it is more similar to the check clearing houses than to the card networks. Although some "small b" brands have evolved ("direct deposit of payroll," and, arguably, "eCheck"), there is no ACH equivalent of an acceptance mark such as "Visa" or "NYCE." Despite this lack of branding, the system has shown robust growth, by providing an efficient set of "rails" for banks and their customers to use.

Why ACH is Different

Why is NACHA's role so limited, when the ACH network is so pervasive? The answer—of course—is money. Banks using the ACH network do not pay a "tax" to NACHA (comparable to the card network assessments). As a result, NACHA does not have the resources for product development, brand advertising, or network expansion that the card networks do. One could argue, of course, that the reason the card networks can charge such a "tax" is because of the direct revenues (interest, interchange, fees) that the banks earn on issuing card products.

The ACH system has no end-party brands similar to those in the card payments systems. Some "small-b" brands (e.g., direct deposit of payroll) have been established through common usage. Other terms (e.g., "eCheck") have not yet achieved that status.

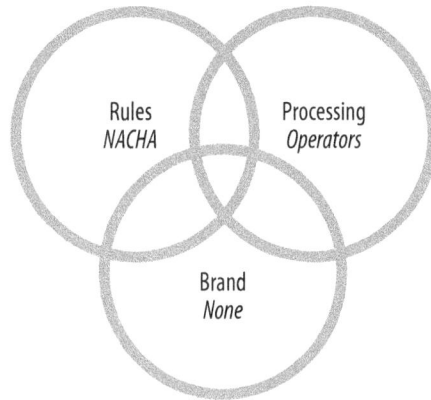

Figure 4-2: ACH— Where's the Brand?

ACH Regulation

ACH transactions are governed both by private NACHA rules and by Federal Reserve Bank regulation.

The NACHA rules bind the ODFIs, the RDFIs, and the ACH operators. Originators, receivers, and third-party service providers are bound by contractual agreements with their ODFIs and/or RDFIs. NACHA rules are voted on by members of NACHA: the larger banks, which belong directly to NACHA, and the regional associations, who represent smaller banks through their membership in NACHA.

ACH rules specify some of the provisions of these downstream contracts, and fall into three groups:

- Rules that apply to all ACH transactions
- Rules that apply to ACH Debit ("pull") transactions or ACH Credit ("push") transactions
- Rules that apply to only certain ACH types, defined by the Standard Entry Class (SEC) Code

ACH operators have private rules that bind ODFIs and RDFIs using their services. These rules are very narrow in scope relative to the ACH rules. For example, banks that use the Federal Reserve Bank as an operator are subject to Operating Circular 4.

In addition to these private rules, U.S. law applies to many types of ACH transactions:

- Regulation E of the Federal Reserve Bank, implementing the Electronic Fund Transfer Act, applies to consumer transactions. Regulation E is the key regulation that specifies consumers' right to return unauthorized transactions.

- U.C.C. 4 and 4a apply to ACH corporate credit transfers.
- Federal government ACH transactions are regulated by the Treasury Department.

If there is a conflict in rules, obviously, U.S. law prevails over private association rules. This means that NACHA must ensure that any new U.S. law or regulation is either correctly reflected in the ACH rules, or at least not contradicted. This has become increasingly complex—partly because of check-to-ACH conversion, and partly because of increasingly expansive federal law and regulation around consumer rights.

Uses of the ACH System

The ACH system is broadly used for many types of payments. Both large and small enterprises, including corporations, governments, and nonprofits, use the ACH to make payments to, and to collect payments from, consumers. Enterprises also use the ACH to make payments to each other, and to transfer funds within a company. In the card payments systems, merchant acquirers use ACH to credit merchants with funds from their card payment activity.

ACH volumes have grown steadily since inception. In recent years, there has been particularly strong growth of the WEB transaction type, an ad-hoc transaction initiated from DDA information entered through an online website. ACH transactions are classified with transaction codes, called SECs or Standard Entry Codes, specifying transaction type. The SEC transaction code is included in every transaction, giving the ACH system detail about the uses of the system that some other payments systems cannot offer. A full list of SEC codes is available through NACHA.

The table below lists common ACH transaction types and codes.

Type of Payment	Authorization	Codes	Uses
Business to consumer	Preauthorized, standing instruction	PPD Credit	Payroll, benefits
Consumer to business	Preauthorized, standing instruction	PPD Debit	Bill payment
Business to business	One-time	CCD Credits and Debits, CTX	Supplier payments, intra-company payments
Consumer to business	One-time	TEL, WEB Debit, POS, CIE	Bill payment, purchases, transfers
Consumer to consumer	One-time	WEB Credit	Person-to-person payments

Table 4-2: ACH Transaction Types

Preauthorized Consumer Transactions

- PPD (prearranged payment and deposit) Credit transactions are used for payroll, pension, and benefit payments to consumers.

- PPD Debit transactions are used primarily for recurring bill payments from consumers.

- These two transaction types built early volume for the ACH, and growth in both categories has been steady over its history. Both require consumers to preauthorize transactions.

Business-to-Business Transactions

- CCD (corporate credit or debit) Credit transactions are used for supplier payments, in lieu of checks. CCD Debit transactions may also be used for supplier payments, for example, when a corporate customer gives a trusted supplier the ability to debit its account. When suppliers are paid with CCD transactions, the customer frequently must send remittance data (explaining details of the payment) separately by mail, fax, or email.

- CCD Debit transactions are frequently used for intracompany funds concentration. A corporation with bank accounts in multiple states, for example, may use the ACH to pull funds into a single account for investment. CCD Debits are also used for government tax collections.

- CTX (corporate trade exchange) Credit transactions are similar to those via CCD Credit, but are designed to carry addenda records with each financial transaction. This allows a corporate customer to pay a supplier and send remittance data along with the payment; the RDFI is required to provide the data it receives to the receiving corporation.

Check Conversion Transactions

Beginning in 2001, NACHA, in cooperation with the Federal Reserve Bank (in its regulatory role with respect to Regulation E), approved a series of new ACH transaction codes to implement check conversion. The permitted situations vary by category listed below, but have certain parameters in common. As shown in the figure below, each transaction begins when someone writes a paper check. When that check is given to the payee, the payee, in cooperation with its bank, creates a new ACH transaction to replace the check. The original check is destroyed and the ACH transaction is carried through the ACH network to effect a debit at the check writer's bank. The payment ceases being governed by check law and regulation, and is instead governed by ACH rules and regulation.

The ARC service is offered to a biller by its lockbox bank. Checks are scanned, and an ACH file created from MICR line data and the dollar amount. The ACH debit transaction is forwarded to the bank's ACH operator. The check is destroyed after a brief retention period.

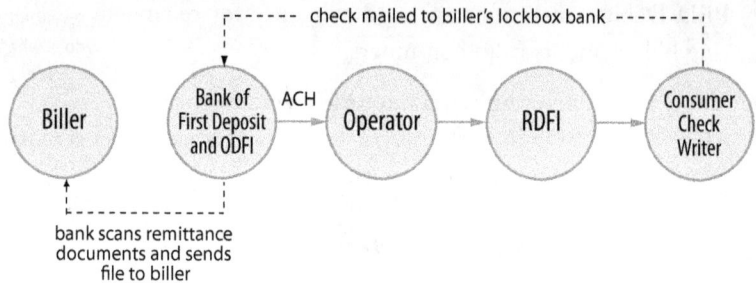

Figure 4-3: ACH Check Conversion

Maintaining Bank Account Information

Although checks remain the predominant form of supplier payments in the United States, business-to-business ACH transactions have grown steadily.

One challenge is that the paying enterprise must collect and maintain bank account information (transit routing number and account number) for each supplier it pays.

• ARC (accounts receivable conversion) transactions occur when a consumer check is received at a bank lockbox that is serving a biller. With the agreement of the biller, the check is converted to an ACH transaction. The consumer is notified passively (for example, by a notice in a statement "stuffer"); the consumer's positive consent is not required.

• POP (point of purchase) transactions occur when a consumer check is presented at a cash register point of sale. The clerk takes the check, runs it through the register to capture the MICR data, and returns the check to the consumer, stamped as void. The register then generates the ACH transaction to debit the consumer's account. (The POP transaction, not surprisingly, created some initial confusion among consumers—"Why am I getting my check back?")

• BOC (back-office conversion) transactions occur when a consumer provides a check at either a point of sale or a biller location. As the name implies, the actual conversion occurs not in front of the consumer, but in the originator's (or ODFI's) back office. Notice to the consumer that BOC will occur must be posted at the point of sale or other check-receiving location.

Most business-to-business checks and government-to-consumer checks are not yet eligible for conversion to ACH.

One-time Consumer Transactions

This group of transactions is the focus of much interest in the payments community. Although, like the check conversion transactions above, they are often referred to as "eChecks," these transactions do not start as checks—they start as "native electronic" ACH transactions. The important difference between these transactions and the PPD debit transactions described above is that, as the name implies, consumers do not preauthorize ad hoc transactions with an assumption of ongoing use. Rather, they can be used for one-time consumer transactions. The consumer's authorization is still very important, particularly since these transactions (like all ACH consumer debit transactions) are covered by ACH rules and Reg E provisions, which ensure that a consumer can refuse an unauthorized transaction.

WEB transaction: On its website, the biller offers the consumer an option to pay "using your bank account." The consumer enters his or her bank routing and account numbers and authorizes the transaction.

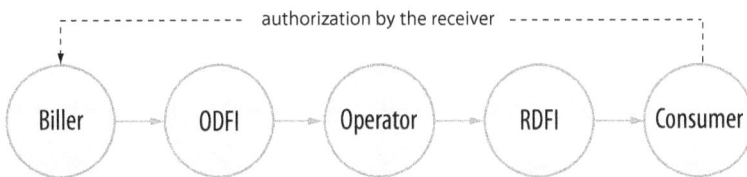

The biller is liable for the validity of this authorization; the consumer's right to repudiate unauthorized transactions is mandated by Federal Reserve Board Regulation E. The ODFI is responsible to the network for the biller's compliance. The biller, of course, is also subject to good-funds risk, as the debit may "bounce" for insufficient funds.

Figure 4-4: ACH WEB Transactions

- An ACH WEB transaction, as shown above, is authorized by a consumer, over the Internet. Its primary uses are bill payment, eCommerce purchases, and account-to-account transfers. A consumer making an online payment is shown an option such as "pay from your bank account"; he or she then enters a bank routing number and account number. The biller or merchant, in the role of originator, then takes a batch of similar transactions and passes them to its ODFI.

  Mechanically, this is the same process used for any ACH Debit transaction. The potential risks are considerably higher, however: a consumer could enter another person's bank account information, and the fraud (or error) might not be caught until that other person saw the incorrect debit on his or her bank account. Reg E establishes a "60 days from date of statement receipt" window for the consumer to repudiate the debit—effectively putting the ODFI, and its originator customer, at risk for up to 90 days. Despite this potential risk, actual return rates on WEB transactions are quite low, apparently evidencing sound work on authenticating the transactions on the part of the originator and the ODFI.

WEB transactions are also used by third-party payments services such as PayPal. Typically, the third-party payments service structures a two-part payment. As an example, consider an eCommerce purchase. The payments service pays the eCommerce merchant directly; most typically, this is an ACH credit transaction in which the payments service is the originator. The second transaction occurs when the payments service, again acting as originator, submits a WEB debit transaction to pull funds from the consumer's account.

The third party in the example above is at extreme risk if the consumer transaction is fraudulent—e.g., if the consumer has given someone else's bank account information. To manage this risk, PayPal early on developed a "micro deposit" scheme designed to verify account ownership. By making two small, random deposits in the consumer's bank account, and then asking the consumer to report the amounts, PayPal can verify that the consumer that controls the demand deposit account is the same consumer that controls the PayPal account. Other users of WEB transactions have followed PayPal in this approach to verification. This tactic protects the originator (and therefore the ODFI) from most fraud risk but does not, of course, cover the NSF risk.

- The "TEL" transaction code is used just like the WEB Debit transaction, with the consumer's authorization, obviously, being obtained by telephone rather than online.

- The CIE (Customer Initiated Entry) transaction code is used when a bank initiates a bill payment transaction, on an individual transaction basis, to effect a consumer bill payment. It should be noted, however, that most online bank bill payment doesn't work this way: rather, the consumer's bank debits the consumers account (with an "on-us" credit to the bank's clearing account), and then initiates a CCD payment to the biller—paying for a group of consumers in aggregate—or, at times, by writing a check to the biller.

- The POS transaction code is used for purchases at the point of sale that are authorized on a one-time basis by a consumer. The POS transaction type is still small in terms of transaction volume, but holds a great deal of promise—and interest—in the payments community. Here, the consumer is not remote, but present at a physical point of sale. The merchant, acting as an originator, creates a one-time consumer debit transaction. The merchant must obtain consumer authorization, and faces the same challenge in verifying bank account information as does the originator of a WEB Debit. Merchants (and third-party payment providers) use a wide range of authentication schemes, many involving cards (a payment-enabling supermarket loyalty card, for example, or a driver's license) to capture the payment instruction. The mobile phone is an obvious potential expansion of this concept.

- WEB Credits, introduced in 2013, allow an originator to initiate a one-time credit transfer to another consumer.

International Transactions

- IAT is the transaction code for all international ACH transactions. Although the transactions themselves are not international, as both ODFI and RDFI are U.S. chartered financial institutions, it is used when the ODFI knows that the transaction is coming from or destined for another country. The IAT code was put in place to help both ODFI's and RDFI's manage their compliance requirements under OFAC.

> **It's Not Just Money**
>
> NACHA has been increasingly active in enabling and promoting the use of the ACH network to carry payments-related data, as well as payments instructions. The CTX transaction type pioneered this, with the use of addenda records to carry business remittance data. Since then, NACHA has sponsored the Electronic Billing Information Delivery (EBID) protocol, to enable billers to deliver bill data to banks (which then provide them to consumers via online banking), triggering, typically, a CIE bill payment. Recent NACHA rules changes enable passing 80 characters of payment related information in free form text along with a person-to-person payment (the new WEB Credit transaction type).

> **Who Controls the ACH?**
>
> Although banks control ACH rules (by voting, directly or through membership in regional ACH associations), at times it has seemed that rules are approved which are contrary to bank interests. Most dramatically, the 2001 approval of the WEB transaction code, which enabled a highly successful large-scale migration of bill payments from check to electronics—also enabled an unanticipated and arguably bank-unfriendly use of the system. Third-party payments services providers, most notably PayPal, used the transaction code to pull inexpensive ACH Debit transactions to fund eCommerce purchases by their customers. This meant, in some situations, that the ACH transaction took the place of what would have been a more profitable debit card transaction for the consumer's bank. This has been the source of some controversy in the industry. As a result, bankers responsible for ACH rule decisions have become increasingly cautious, hoping to avoid additional encounters with the "law of unintended consequences."

Risk Management

Users and providers of ACH services are exposed to a number of risks that must be managed:

- ODFIs are liable for the actions of their originating clients. In particular, authorization from the underlying receiver is often the responsibility of the originator; this responsibility is carried to the ODFI. This is critically important with ACH Debit (pull) transactions. If either the identity of the underlying receiver is wrong (for example, A uses B's name fraudulently) or the bank account information is wrong (B gives C's bank account information by mistake), the ODFI is financially responsible. Obviously, an ODFI will pass on that responsibility to the originator in its contract; however, if the originator is a small or financially unstable company, it may not be able to repay the ODFI.

- RDFIs must accurately post transactions. If the transaction is an ACH Debit (pull) transaction, the RDFI must handle returns for NSF or disputed transactions according to a specified timeline.

- Merchants and billers originating ACH Debits must manage the risk that transactions will be returned for NSF or, for consumer transactions, for lack of authorization—this latter dispute can happen as late as 60 days after the consumer's receipt of a statement or notification from his or her bank.

- Businesses must carefully manage bank accounts to ensure that no fraudulent ACH Debit transactions are posted (as they must with checks as well). Importantly, a business receiving an unauthorized ACH Debit does not have the Reg E protections that a consumer has.

Economics

The ACH system was designed as a low-cost, widely used utility for banks and their customers. It has largely succeeded in that goal: the cost—for enterprises and consumers—of using the system is very low, as is the cost—to bankers and processors—of providing the system. There is no interchange in the ACH system, and no float or lending revenue directly related to it.

ACH Products

ACH Origination

Banks and third parties compete for corporate ACH origination business, including payroll, preauthorized debits, business-to-business transactions, and the various "eChecks." Large corporations transmit batch files of transactions to their ODFIs; both small and large corporations may also execute smaller numbers of ACH transactions over online systems provided by a bank or a third party.

Total fee and fee equivalent revenue to banks for origination is considerably less than the revenue associated, for example, with credit card issuance. Pricing to corporate originators varies by size of enterprise and type of transaction. A very high-volume payroll file, for example, might be priced at pennies per transaction. A lower-volume B2B transaction might be priced at 50 cents or a dollar per transaction.

ACH origination is often sold as part of a package of specialized services, such as these:

- Payroll. Banks and third parties compete to provide payroll services to enterprises of all sizes. Services often include management of tax calculations and withholdings as well as check issuance, ACH origination, and employee reporting and service.

- Retail lockbox. Banks and third parties compete to manage inbound consumer bill payments by check. The same entities often support receipt of preauthorized ACH payments for bill payment, and the conversion of checks received into ACH ARC (accounts receivable) debits.

- Wholesale lockbox. Banks and third parties compete to manage inbound business remittances by check, ACH, and wire. Remittance data handling is a key part of this service—it may include manual data entry (for remittance data coming with checks) and reformatting of data received with ACH transactions. To date, there is little conversion to ACH of business-to-business checks.

- Supplier payments. Banks and third parties compete to handle outbound business remittances to suppliers. These services may include printing checks and associated remittance data, preparing ACH transactions, and managing outbound remittance data through a variety of channels, including ACH (CTX), mail, fax, email, transmission to third-party value-added networks, etc. More advanced services could include collection and management of electronic invoices or maintenance of supplier databases.

- Retail payment acceptance. Banks, card acquirers, and other third parties compete to offer services to retailers receiving checks at the point of sale. These services may include conversion of the check to an ACH item or presentment of the check by image. Item verification or guarantee may be part of this offering. As point of sale ACH services mature, it is logical that the same providers will offer this service to merchants.

Banks and third parties often incorporate ACH origination into a package of services, bundled with value-added services (e.g., state tax calculations sold along with payroll payments).

ACH Receipt

Banks and third parties rarely charge consumers for receipt of an ACH transaction, i.e., for acting as an RDFI. Businesses, particularly small businesses, are often charged to receive ACH transactions from their clients.

ACH Expenses

Bank Processing and Clearing

Banks tend to run ACH operations centers as cost centers that support multiple areas of the bank—both the consumer accounts organization, for example, and the corporate payments organization might use the same ACH "engine." Medium and large banks buy specialized software that allows them to process both ACH originations and receipts. Smaller banks may outsource part or all of their ACH operations to processors.

Banks remove "on-us" ACH transactions submitted by originators and post those transactions directly to the receiver's account. The bank then sends the remaining origination transactions to its ACH operator, which sorts the transactions and sends them on to either the RDFI (if both use the same operator) or to another operator, as appropriate. Operators charge for both receipt and delivery of ACH batches—costs are dependent on volume—but, at high volumes, are in fractions of a penny per transaction.

Historically, bank ACH operations were relatively inexpensive to run, particularly when most transactions were preauthorized consumer debits and credits. For banks, the proliferation of new transaction types, each with its own risk management and compliance considerations, has increased the cost of managing the ACH process—offset, in part, by revenue from new services and products.

One challenging element is the RDFI's management of disputed consumer transactions. The RDFI receives no compensation for an inbound PPD Debit or WEB transaction. If a consumer disputes a transaction, the RDFI bears the costs of managing the dispute—which can often exceed the value of the transaction itself. (This process also occurs in checking—but banks have found the electronic ACH process simpler and less costly.)

ACH Trends

Same Day ACH

In 2015, NACHA passed a significant new rule for the ACH system. "Same Day" ACH enables any ODFI, acting on behalf of its originator, to send a batch of ACH transactions which will settle among the two banks that same day. Significantly, the protocol requires all RDFI's to accept these transactions—meaning that the all-important attribute of "ubiquity" (the ability to reach any bank account) is met. All common ACH transactions except for IAT (International) transactions can be same day, although there is a $25,000 limit on the amount of individual transactions. Same day ACH will have a phased introduction: starting in September 2016 for ACH credits ("push" payments), expanding to credits and debits ("pull" payments) in September 2017. Funds need to be available in the recipient's account by the end of the RDFI's business day; by March 2018 both credits and debits need to be made available at the RDFI by 5pm local time.

A very significant part of same day ACH is the institution of ACH interchange on these transactions. The ODFI will pay the RDFI a flat fee of $.052 (NACHA calls this a "Same Day Entry Fee") per transaction. This was apparently necessary in order to get the thousands of small participating RDFI's to agree to the new rule—which will require them to invest in new processing capabilities.

Same day ACH is an important step forward for the ACH system, but it is equally important to understand what it is not—it is not an "immediate funds transfer" system. Same day ACH relies on the same batch processing protocols that are used in "normal" ACH transactions.

ACH "Cards"

Just as there are private label credit cards, there are also private label debit cards. Private label debit cards are given to consumers by a store or other business. The cards use card network account numbering schemes and follow mag stripe and chip configurations to allow them to be processed by stores' POS machines. But transactions are sent, not to the card networks, but rather to the store's ODFI, who creates a POS ACH Debit transaction to "pull" the money from the cardholder's account. The store (or their service provider) assumes the risk of insufficient funds ("bouncing") and of fraud. In exchange, the store pays only a low, flat fee (perhaps several cents), instead of a card merchant discount fee. The attractiveness of ACH cards to stores was diminished after the enactment of Regulation II (the Durbin Amendment), which drastically lowered the cost of large bank debit card transactions.

ACH cards are not to be confused with "decoupled debit" cards. In 2007, Capital One issued a controversial card product which it referred to as a "decoupled debit" card: the card carried a Mastercard network brand, making it usable wherever those cards are accepted, but the funding was done through an ACH debit. The product was not successful and was withdrawn from the market.

> ### *Faster Payments*
>
> In the UK, the banks have implemented a new core payments system, "Faster Payments," which is a real-time immediate funds transfer system. It uses a net settlement model to settle on a same-day basis multiple times per day. It is used for push payments, particularly person-to-person, bill-pay, and business-to-business transactions. Many other countries are implementing similar systems.
>
> In the United States, multiple networks are competing for this role, including networks being built by The Clearing House, and existing networks controlled by Early Warning Services, Visa, Mastercard, Fiserv, and FIS. The Federal Reserve has taken a leadership role in fostering faster payments in the U.S. through a Faster Payments Task Force established in 2015.

International Transactions

Although the ACH system is not international, both ACH operators and the ACH rules support the concept of links between the ACH system and other similar payments systems in other countries. Some early users were corporations paying retirees or employees in other countries. The Fed, acting as an ACH operator, established links to countries such as Canada and the UK to handle credit ("push") payments under the product name "Fed Global."

Businesses also began to use these links for cross-border supplier payments. Because these types of transactions involve more than one payments system, considerable difficulties are associated with timing, risk management, settlement (especially foreign exchange management), and data formats. Increasing attention has been given to the need to comply with laws, in the U.S. and other jurisdictions, designed to combat money laundering and other criminal activities. The IAT transaction code was implemented in 2009 in order to help manage these risks.

An international group of banks, ACH systems, and processors are working on the IPFA (International Payments Framework Association) framework to enable cross-border ACH to work without the need for country-by-country bilateral arrangements.

ACH Economics—Under the Interchange Umbrella

Merchants, billers, and other receivers receiving payment via credit or debit card are used to paying a merchant discount fee—a blend of fixed and percentage costs determined in large part by the card network's interchange fee schedule. For such receivers of funds, ACH offers the opportunity for a dramatic cost reduction. An eCommerce merchant selling a $100 item might pay $2.50 in discount fees if a credit card is used, vs. perhaps pennies if an ACH "eCheck" is used. Against this economic benefit, the merchant would have to weigh the cost of returns—will the transaction be denied by the consumer as fraudulent or will the transaction bounce for insufficient funds? At least two economic models are being formed for such ACH transactions: one in which the receiver (merchant or biller) bears those risks, and one in which a third party assumes some or all of the risk for the recipient. If a third party bears risk, the cost of the transaction to the merchant will, of course, go up.

Major Providers

Because of the reach of the ACH system, there is a large ecosystem of providers that are involved in some way in ACH origination, receipt, or processing. Many bank and processors embed ACH capabilities in with other payments products.

- NACHA sets, develops, and enforces adherence to ACH rules and handles much of the definition of new product and transaction types.

NACHA balances the needs of small financial institutions—some of which are only RDFIs—with the needs of larger ODFIs.

- The Federal Reserve Bank is pivotal in ACH, playing three roles: as regulator, as one of the two large-scale ACH operators, and as the provider of settlement services.

- The Clearing House owns EPN, the other large-scale ACH operator.

- Local payments associations—formerly local automated clearing houses—often operate on a regional basis; they serve as their depository financial institution's connection to NACHA, and also as a source of industry education.

- ACH processing software vendors and service providers. All of the large bank "core processors" provide ACH receipt and origination service for their clients.

- The large originating banks, which invest heavily in ACH capabilities in order to support corporate origination of transactions. NACHA publishes transaction volumes of ODFIs on an annual basis.

- Large originators make their voices heard through their ODFIs and directly to NACHA through a series of councils run by NACHA. Though the councils do not have rule-making powers, both banks and non-banks can participate, and councils have representatives on the NACHA board. The AFP (Association of Finance Professionals), representing enterprise financial requirements, also provides a forum for enterprise input on ACH issues.

- The U.S. government is an active user and supporter of the ACH system, and follows the NACHA operating rules.

Summary: ACH

Key Trends in ACH

The simplicity, broad reach, and economic efficiency of the ACH system make it one of the most important electronic transfer systems in the country. The unique capability of the ACH system to carry large amounts of data along with a payment transaction is enabling interesting new applications, particularly in bill payment and B2B transactions. The ACH system will, however, face continuing competition with better-branded card payments systems that enable different economic models for their providers.

- Increasing pressure for faster settlement, and a parallel (but different) developing demand for real-time payments are increasing. These demands may be met by the ACH, or by other systems, which will compete with the ACH.

- Growth and complexity: overall, ACH volumes continue to grow and transaction types proliferate. Banks are increasing investment to manage the complexity.

- New ACH transaction types are enabling new forms of commerce and payment, but also increasing risk.

- ACH has been a behind-the-scenes enabler for "alternative payments" providers in the online space. Now ACH is poised to play the same role at the point of sale and for mobile payments.

- International ACH volumes are increasing, and new compliance requirements are focusing attention on these transactions.

Sources of Information—ACH

- PaymentsNews.com
- NACHA
- Regional ACH payments associations
- The Federal Reserve Bank Retail Payments Office

Core Systems: Cards

Type	"Pull payments" payments with authorization
Ownership	Private network ownership – public companies
Regulation	Network rules; U.S. law and Federal Reserve Bank regulation
Network Economics	Interchange (acquirers to issuers), assessments (issuers and acquirers to network), currency conversion on cross-currency
Processing	Electronic
Risk Management	Defined by card networks and augmented by processors and end parties

Table 5-1: Cards Overview

The card payments systems fascinate many people, within financial services and in many other industries, because they are at the heart of consumer commerce—facilitating trillions of dollars of consumer and business spending each year. The card systems are especially significant because of their sheer size, the extent of their global reach, their staggering degree of standardization and interoperability (enabling a cardholder from Topeka, Kansas to walk into a bar in Singapore and buy a drink, no questions asked), and, perhaps most significantly, the fabulous profits that have flowed, in particular, to credit card issuers over the years—but also to other participants in the payments cards value chain.

History and Background

The payments cards industry has its roots in the private department store and oil company "credit cards" issued during the first half of the 20th century. Later, the charge cards issued by Diners Club and American Express in the 1950s, primarily intended for business travel and entertainment (T&E) purposes, established the early "closed loop" card systems.

The card industry as we know it today, however, began in 1966, when Bank of America formed a company, BankAmerica Service Corporation, to franchise its BankAmericard product to other banks. Bank of America had launched BankAmericard in the late 1950s, planning to roll it out across California; in the mid-1960s it began licensing BankAmericard to other banks located outside of California and in a handful of other countries. By 1970, the franchisees began pressing for a new organizational structure for the product, leading to the formation of National BankAmericard Inc. (NBI) to manage the U.S. card program. In the mid-1970s, a similar organization was formed to manage the international card program. Shortly thereafter, the two organizations came together under a new company named Visa—with the international organization (IBANCO) becoming Visa International and NBI becoming Visa USA, a group member of Visa International.

Separately, and in competition with Bank of America's card program, another group of California banks formed a competing organization called the Interbank Card Association (ICA). The ICA created Master Charge: The Interbank Card and, in 1979, renamed itself and its products to Mastercard.

The early work done by these new companies, structured as associations of member financial institutions, was nothing short of remarkable. They established the principles of open financial institution membership—the open-loop exchange of transactions, interchange fees, and brand control through association bylaws and operating rules that would, over time, grow to define the card payments systems.

Significantly, these rules set the groundwork for interoperability that quickly grew global, as card systems were developed in other countries and linked into the Visa and Mastercard systems to extend their scope of coverage. Interoperability was primarily technical, of course, establishing protocols and timelines for all aspects of issuance, acceptance, and transaction management, but the card associations also defined the system economics, brand management, and requirements for transaction interchange.

Over time, the card associations played important roles in managing card fraud—requiring that confirmed fraud be reported by issuers to the associations and using that confirmed fraud "outcome data" to build increasingly sophisticated data analytics systems to help fight it.

The associations also established arbitration processes for the resolution of disputes between members—ensuring that any such disputes would be resolved "within the family," with association staff acting as court, judge, and jury.

Membership

Membership in the open-loop associations was strictly limited to banks and other regulated depository financial institutions. Global and regional associations defined their own criteria for admission, related to capital adequacy—a member bank must be able to meet its daily funding liabilities to the network, and hence to other members. In many countries, the associations relied on existing bank regulatory and supervision infrastructures to effectively handle this task. In the association bylaws, each board of directors set membership voting rights, seeking to balance the needs of small and large participants and giving some "early owner" benefits to founding members.

In joining the card associations, member banks surrendered considerable individual control over how these products worked—but gained the significant benefits of common product definitions and a global acceptance framework that no one bank could develop on its own. Ultimately, some large banks found it frustrating to see the card association brands become stronger and more visible to consumers than the banks' own brands.

Why did banks agree to participate in these associations? The answer is almost entirely economic. The open-loop networks, in their early credit card days, enabled a very profitable consumer lending business for card-issuing banks. Originally intended as a means for allowing banks to efficiently, and profitably, lend to their own existing customers, the credit card quickly opened up, for imaginative banks, a new way to extend lending to consumers outside of a bank's existing geographic footprint. New and profitable customer relationships could be established—on the basis not of a consumer opening a checking account but, rather, applying for a credit card from the bank.

These economics also explain the relative power of card issuing banks (serving consumers) vs. acquiring banks (serving merchants) within the card networks. Although originally most banks were both issuers and acquirers, card acquiring was not nearly as profitable as card issuing. The different economic models of these two sides of the card business led many banks to separate management of card issuing and acquiring, with many banks dropping out of the card acquiring business in the 1980s, after the acceptance environment evolved from paper-based (requiring local capture of paper sales drafts using a process similar to checks) to electronic POS terminals. On the critical operating committees and boards of the card associations, the voice of card issuers frequently dominated discussions. This continues today even within the new ownership structure of the open-loop networks as they continue to focus primarily on the needs of their card issuer clients. More recently, both Visa and Mastercard have increased their efforts to try to work more closely with merchants even in the face of protracted court battles over issues relating to operating rules and interchange fees.

Fundamentally, the card lifecycle for a card network begins with issuance and, thus, a network's primary focus is on gaining issuance of cards by their issuing bank partners that use the network's brand. In the U.S., "duality" has been the practice of issuing banks for many years—issuing both Visa and Mastercard cards. Both card networks have pursued stronger partnership relationships with issuers—especially the larger issuers—as they seek to gain increased commitment to issuance of their brand over competitors. As part of those relationships, the networks may provide various incentives to their partner issuers to help secure their commitment to their network.

ATM and Debit Network Formation

In the late 1960s—and in parallel with the growth of credit cards—banks began to introduce automated teller machines (ATMs) as a new channel for serving checking account customers. Banks issued ATM cards to their customers so they could access the ATMs for cash withdrawals. Usage of these cards required individual personal identification numbers (PINs) to authenticate the cardholder at the ATM—as it was an unattended card acceptance location with no clerk on hand to compare physical signatures on the back of card and the signed receipt.

> **Double Innovation?**
>
> It is interesting to note that at about the time the ATM networks were being formed, the same departments within the same banks had people working on the fledgling ACH system. At the time, the new networks were responding to very different needs: cash dispensing vs. check replacement, respectively. Now, however, the two "grown-up" networks compete for many types of transactions.

Eventually, retail bank organizations within major banks began forming shared networks to interconnect ATMs and banks within cities and geographic regions. Although similar in some respects to the credit card open-loop associations, the shared ATM networks had entirely different economic frameworks—their members were much more motivated by cost reduction (e.g., saving on branch teller expense) than by profit. After all, ATMs weren't consumer lending tools—they simply provided a more convenient channel for customers to access the cash in their checking account and helped eliminate some of the labor associated with accepting deposits and making cash available in bank branches.

> **VISA Debit Strategy**
>
> Following the migration from paper-based acceptance to electronic acceptance, Visa believed that debit cards were going to become increasingly important for merchant acceptance. Unsure of how the debit card market might evolve, Visa hedged its bets—by providing processing services and ultimately acquiring Interlink, by becoming an ACH operator (briefly), and by enhancing its credit card network to better meet the needs of consumers and banks for debit card products.

In the late 1980s and 1990s, the shared ATM networks went through a series of mergers, with a handful of large national networks emerging; Interlink, STAR, and NYCE were among the largest. A number of smaller regional networks continue to exist, most operating on an association, non-profit basis.

By and large, the U.S. credit card associations were not involved in these early ATM networks. However, Visa, in particular, was watching their development—particularly when the ATM networks began extending acceptance of their bank-issued ATM cards to new merchant locations (especially supermarkets and fuel retailers). Once again, banks were interested in the potential cost savings from having their ATM cards accepted at the point of sale with these kinds of merchants instead of checks.

Similarly, merchants appreciated the elimination of checks and their associated insufficient funds "bounce" risk, while enjoying the benefits of receiving a guaranteed payment when an ATM card was used instead. The shared ATM/PIN debit networks priced merchant acceptance attractively as an incentive—creating a win-win for merchants, consumers, and banks. But merchants did need to deploy new acceptance equipment at the point of sale—not just to read the card's magnetic stripe, but also to securely accept the cardholder's PIN.

In parallel with this evolution of the ATM networks and their cards, credit card acceptance began transitioning from paper-based to a fully authorized electronic environment beginning in the mid-1980s—and these two different systems for merchant acceptance began increasingly colliding. This led to Visa and Mastercard developing debit products for retail banks that would ride over their credit card network "rails" rather than over the shared ATM/PIN debit networks.

Along the way, Visa began providing processing services to the west coast-based Interlink network, and did so for many years before ultimately acquiring that network from its member banks. In the process, Visa acquired a large ATM/PIN debit network to complement its existing credit card network.

In the early 1990s, after initial efforts by Visa and Mastercard to collaborate on debit cards were blocked by the U.S. Department of Justice, both Visa and Mastercard introduced their own debit card products—these became known as "signature debit cards"—as alternatives to the PIN debit cards for handling debit transactions to a consumer's checking account. The differences between these two types of cards will be discussed in more detail later in this chapter.

Card Lessons—Debit is Different!

When Visa and Mastercard executives went to their member banks to discuss the new debit card products, they quickly learned that they were talking to the wrong people! In most large banks, the powerful managers of the credit card issuing businesses had little to do with the people who ran the branch banking network—the retail bank—and who controlled the ATM and PIN debit networks. Full of plans to roll out PIN debit cards, these retail bank executives were not pleased to hear that their plans for the expansion of merchant acceptance were being hijacked by the much more profitable credit card issuing business unit—their rival within the bank. It took a number of years for banks to sort this out, and to focus on the higher profitability of the Visa and Mastercard products relative to the PIN debit products.

Going Public

Today, the two major U.S. open-loop card networks are no longer owned by banks, but are rather publicly traded companies—a fact that would have astonished a 1980s card banker used to working collaboratively within the association structures of that era.

The first networks to transition to non-bank ownership were the large, shared ATM/PIN debit networks bought by payment processors. In 2004, First Data Corporation bought STAR (through First Data's acquisition of Concord EFS) and Metavante bought NYCE (ironically from First Data, which was required by regulators to sell NYCE after First Data's acquisition of Concord EFS). Banks' willingness to give up control of these networks was largely a matter of cost. The payment processors saw opportunities to participate in increased transaction volumes as debit acceptance continued to expand. As mentioned earlier, the other major, shared ATM/PIN debit network, Interlink, had already been acquired by Visa.

Perhaps the most dramatic change occurred in May 2006 with Mastercard's initial public offering. Later that year, Visa (excepting Visa Europe which opted to remain a separate, bank-owned entity) announced that it would also go public—and followed in March 2008 with what was, up until that point, the largest initial public offering (IPO) in U.S. history. In late 2015, Visa Inc. announced the acquisition of Visa Europe—bringing together the two separate companies into a single global organization.

Member bank agreement to support the two major card associations going public was based upon different reasons than with the earlier sales of shared ATM/PIN debit networks to processors. The Mastercard and Visa IPOs certainly allowed banks to recognize the value of their investments in the two associations, which had previously been carried entirely off banks' balance sheets. But much more significantly, the association restructurings into public companies provided the banks with a new way to deal with potential liabilities related to an increasingly challenging legal and antitrust environment.

With their IPOs now solidly behind them, the card companies are in a position to acquire, and potentially expand their roles into, a number of new lines of business.

An overview of the history of the U.S. payment card industry is provided in the table below.

U.S. Card Industry Evolution				
Formation	**Expansion**	**Segmentation**	**Diversity**	**Digitize**
1960s–1970s	**1980s**	**1990s**	**2000s**	**2010–>**
• Associations • Regional governance • Revolving credit • Role of issuer & acquirer • Systems infrastructure • Interchange economics • "Honor all cards" • Global interoperability	• Consumer adoption of cards • POS Terminals • New acceptance markets • Third-party processors • Systematic fraud mgmt. • Brand competition; affinity cards • Early litigation	• Co-branding • Debit begins • Rewards cards • Product, rate proliferation • Commercial and purchasing cards • eCommerce begins • EMV chip specification • Receivables securitization • Association litigation losses	• Debit Decade • V/MC IPOs • PayPal, eCommerce • Prepaid cards • Decoupled debit • New form factors • Security: PCI-DSS • Payments as a Service • Merchant power strengthens • Durbin debit, network routing	• EMV to U.S. in 2015 • New regs • No signature • Wallets • Acquisitions • NFC payments • Mobile POS • Tablet registers • Tokenization • P2P; Bitcoin • Visa/Chase • Apple Pay • Chase Pay • Walmart Pay

Table 5-2: A Short History of Cards

When we look back at this history, with its many changes in a relatively short period of time, a couple of major events stand out as particularly important:

- The move, in the mid-1980s, away from paper to electronic POS acceptance and authorization of every transaction was a pivotal development for the industry. Before that point, a merchant accepting a card payment created a paper "sales draft" and deposited it, very much like a paper check, at the local bank branch. Authorization was done by voice over the telephone, and floor limits (below which transactions were simply not authorized) were common. The card associations significantly accelerated the shift from paper to electronic acceptance by creating a new, lower "incentive" interchange rate that merchants could benefit from if they installed the new electronic draft capture POS terminals. This approach also marked the beginning of the use of specialized interchange rates (separating paper-based acceptance from electronic POS-based acceptance), which later came to be used by the card associations to tackle the specialized needs of many other vertical acceptance markets.

- Card associations have historically been the subject of litigation and regulatory scrutiny. Their unusual structure—and their practice of setting interchange rates as well as a variety of membership requirements—raised many questions concerning possible violations of antitrust or other commercial law. A detailed review of the many legal cases in the card industry is outside of the scope of this book, but it is interesting to note that in the early decades of the card industry, the card associations won essentially all of the important cases. Beginning in the late 1990s, the card associations began losing several significant cases.

What's Next for the Now-Public Networks?

It is still early to understand the full implications of this ownership change for the U.S. payments industry. But it is logical to assume the following:

The new card companies have very different economic motivations than did their predecessor associations. Before the IPOs, they operated, practically speaking, on a not-for-profit basis—enabling their members and owners, the banks, to generate profits. Today, they are primarily technology-based processing companies, earning revenue from their bank clients (no longer owners) for transaction handling, brand management, and associated services. A debit transaction may be just as profitable for a card network as a credit transaction—which is certainly not true for a bank issuer. Also, although the card companies set interchange fees, they do not receive those fees—in theory, the card companies could be fine if interchange disappeared entirely.

The power of banks to influence operating rules has also changed with this transition—though banks continue to participate in user groups and remain the primary customers of the card companies, they no longer set policy on interchange, brand, or membership. One possibility? Card companies could eventually open up membership to non-banks and, in fact, this has begun to happen in some markets outside the U.S.

Card Types and Brands

Types

Payment cards may be categorized by type, primarily based on timing of funding—before, during, or after the transaction.

- **Charge cards** are non-revolving credit cards: the cardholder pays in full, at the end of the billing period, for all charges incurred during that month.

- **Credit cards** provide the cardholder easy access to a revolving, unsecured line of credit. The cardholder has the option of paying the balance off in full at the end of the billing period, or "revolving" and paying the balance over a period of time based upon terms set by the card issuer.

- **Signature debit cards** (so called because cardholder authentication is based upon signature comparison at the acceptance location) access funds on deposit in the cardholder's checking account at the issuing bank. The debit to the cardholder account occurs on the day of the transaction. In the U.S., signature debit card transactions are carried over either the Visa or the Mastercard network depending upon the bank issuer's choice of card brand. Visa established an early market share lead with bank issuers of signature debit cards through its use of an integrated debit strategy that optionally provided issuers with debit card processing services. More recently, the Durbin Amendment resulting in Federal Reserve Regulation II required debit card issuers to choose two unaffiliated debit card networks for their cards—and allowed merchants to decide which network would be used for each debit transaction.

- **PIN debit cards** (authenticated at the acceptance location by the consumer entering a PIN) also access funds on deposit in the cardholder's checking account at the issuing bank. The debit to the cardholder account occurs either on the day of, or the day after, the transaction. In the U.S., PIN debit card transactions are carried over national, regional, or local PIN debit or ATM networks—with routing based on the bank issuer's choice of network participation and the accepting merchant's choice of network routing. PIN debit cards, drawing on their ATM network origins, also can be used to provide cash back to the consumer at the point of sale.

> **Double Duty**
>
> The same physical card, and the same card number, is typically used for both PIN and signature debit. The card issuer determines whether both authentication methods are supported. When merchants accept debit cards, they can look up the issuer's routing options and determine whether to prompt for PIN or not. For regulated debit cards in the U.S. today, there's no economic advantage for doing so. But, prior to the Durbin Amendment, large merchants often wanted to prompt for PIN where possible so that they could route the transaction over a lower cost PIN debit network. Today, some large merchants continue to prompt for PIN in an attempt to steer the non-regulated debit cards over a PIN debit network.

- **Prepaid cards** access funds from an account, most typically held by the card issuer or—for single merchant cards—by the merchant, that has been pre-funded by the cardholder (or someone acting on behalf of the cardholder, such as the purchaser of a gift card). Closed loop prepaid cards are usable only at the merchant that issued the card. Open-loop, network-branded prepaid cards are typically signature-based and operate over the Visa or Mastercard networks.

Types of Acceptance Environments

Signature-based cards, both credit and debit, work within two primary acceptance environments:

- **Card-present (CP) transactions** occur when a cardholder is physically using his or her card to effect a transaction at some type of terminal—and the terminal is able to electronically capture the card data. Card-present transactions may be at either attended or unattended venues (for example, a kiosk or vending machine). Card network rules usually protect the merchant from fraud risk in a card-present environment—with fraud losses borne by card issuers. Beginning in late 2015, card network rules changed to incent the adoption of EMV chip card technology—with fraud liability shifting from the issuer to the merchant if the merchant has failed to adopt EMV-capable acceptance devices.

- **Card-not-present (CNP) transactions** occur when the cardholder is making a remote purchase—online, by phone, or even by mail order. Card network rules generally do not protect the card-not-present merchant from fraud risk in a card-not-present environment and these merchants bear the risk of losses on fraudulent transactions. The card networks have developed and deployed additional technology—based on a protocol known as 3D Secure—which allows merchants to request the issuer to authenticate the cardholder. When 3D Secure buyer authentication is utilized, any fraud liability shifts from the merchant to the card issuer.

- **PIN debit transactions** have historically been allowed only in card-present environments: PIN debit network rules have required the entry of a PIN into a secure device. This is now changing, as some PIN networks are allowing card-not-present transactions for bill payment (known as "PIN-less debit") and certain types of low fraud risk eCommerce transactions.

Brands

As the table below shows, most major card brands in the United States support most types of cards. American Express, currently with no debit card offering, is an exception. The major PIN debit networks, now owned by payments processors, have also not expanded into credit or charge card offerings.

	Visa	Mastercard	American Express	Discover	STAR, NYCE, Accel
Charge Cards	✓ P-Cards	✓ P-Cards	✓	✓	
Credit Cards	✓	✓	✓	✓	
Signature Debit	✓	✓		✓	
PIN Debit	✓ Interlink	✓ Maestro		✓ Pulse	✓
ATM	✓ Plus	✓ Cirrus	(ATM Sharing Agreements)	✓ Pulse	✓
Prepaid	✓	✓	✓	✓	✓

Table 5-3: Card Brands

Roles and the Value Chain

The card payments value chain, shown below, has two main components: issuing and acquiring. In an open-loop network, an issuing bank serves the cardholder, and an acquiring bank serves the merchant. The card network sits in the middle and manages the electronic exchange of the items, the setting and ongoing management of rules, and some forms of risk management. The card networks also manage the resolution of any disputes between members—providing an arbitration function whose decisions are final and binding on participants.

Open loop card networks connect two separate value chains—the **issuing process** and the **acquiring process**—at the point of sale.

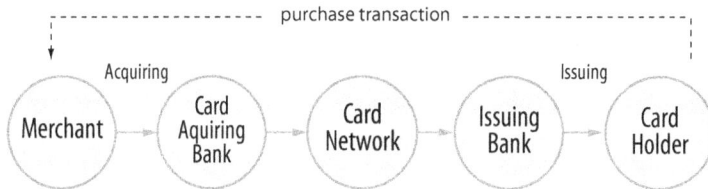

Card processing has a dual message flow: first an authorization message and then a clearing message flow along the same "rails."

Figure 5-1: The Card Payments Value Chain

In a closed loop card model, shown below, the same functions occur, but a single card company performs the issuing, acquiring, and network functions. Hybrid models, in which a closed loop network opens up one side of its network to permit other entities to issue and/or acquire on its behalf, are also evolving as both Discover and American Express have begun pursuing hybrid models.

Closed loop card networks perform the same functions as open loop networks—but the issuing and acquiring functions are done by the network itself (or by a processor on its behalf).

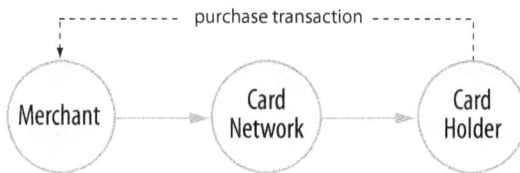

Closed loop networks are more efficient to operate, but may scale more slowly than open loop networks.

Figure 5-2: The Closed Loop Value Chain

Private label cards are a special category of closed loop cards: rather than using a network, these cards are issued by the merchant (or a processor acting on behalf of the merchant), and are accepted only at that merchant's outlets.

Credit card issuance is a term that is easy to understand. The card issuer solicits new consumers, receives and underwrites applications to acquire new customers, furnishes each customer with a card, authorizes and clears card transactions, and provides ongoing statements to cardholders, collections, and customer service.

Card acquiring, on the other hand, is one of the least understood parts of the payments industry. Acquiring is best understood as a set of functions provided to card-accepting merchants, often by different companies, with varying degrees of functional "bundling." In the broadest sense, acquiring refers to functions supporting all of a merchant's needs in card payments acceptance, including POS terminals, software, card processing, dispute management, and merchant customer service. Acquirers want to provide their merchants with support for the card tender types the merchants want to accept. In the narrow and most formal sense, it refers to the requirement, in an open-loop network, that the merchant submit and receive transactions to the network through a contract with a bank that is a member of that network and bound by its operating rules. In practice, the term "acquiring" can include all or only some of these functions.

The functional value chain for debit cards is essentially the same as the value chain for credit or charge cards. Cards are issued, authorized, and cleared over one of the debit networks. The difference between signature debit and PIN debit cards relates primarily to which networks the transactions are processed on, the merchant acceptance environment (PIN-capable or not), and the rules applied by those networks (including interchange).

As the figure below shows, processors are very important in the card payments systems. Processors handle "on behalf of" functions for both issuers and acquirers. The processing industry is much more concentrated than the banking industry as the industry has evolved around a few large processors. Processors generally are more visible on the acquiring side of the business—where they may be the entity a merchant contracts with—than on the issuing side of the business, where they tend to act behind the scenes serving card issuers.

A processor may perform some or most of the functions of an acquiring or issuing bank. Frequently, physical message switching is conducted entirely among banks, processors, and card networks. On the acquiring side, the processor may be the one entity visible to the merchant, and may be considered to be the "acquirer" by the marketplace. There is always an acquiring bank, however, and this bank bears responsibility to the card network for the transaction.

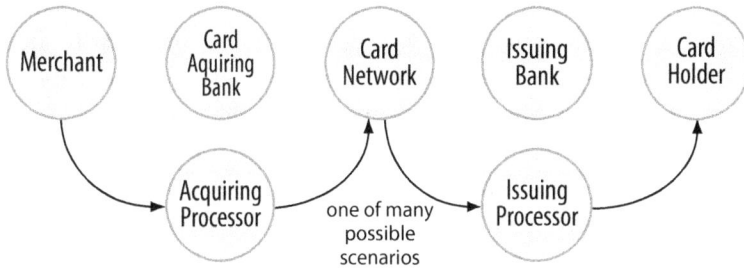

Figure 5-3: Card Processing

Enabling Technology and Standards

Card networks work because the networks and their member banks have agreed on global standards for physical formatting of cards and definition of key data fields.

The Physical Card

American Express first introduced the plastic credit card in 1959—and since that time the dimensions and other physical characteristics of the card has been standardized through industry collaboration as ISO/IEC 7810.

The card has defined data fields and locations, both printed or embossed on the physical card and encoded in the magnetic stripe on its back. Although there are variations by card network, region, and country, enough of the data fields are standardized—or commonly recognized—to enable global interoperability of the system.

> ***Sponsorship Required***
>
> With open-loop networks, the bank itself—either the issuing or the acquiring bank—is always the entity responsible for the transaction to the network. The processor is always sponsored by a member bank in the network. Sometimes, the bank is large and the processor is simply its "hired hand." At other times, the processor is large and visible in the market, and has, in essence, hired the bank to be the sponsor. In either case, however, the ultimate technical and financial responsibility for compliance with card network rules and other regulations remains with the bank.

The key card data element is the PAN, or Primary Account Number. The first six digits of the PAN are the IIN, or Issuer Identification Number, which identifies both the card network and the issuing bank. Earlier these digits were called the BIN, or Bank Identification Number. The American Bankers Association acts as the registration authority for IINs and manages the allocation of IINs to issuers. The PAN is both embossed on the card itself and encoded onto two "tracks" of the magnetic stripe.

A data element, referred to as CVN (Card Verification Number), is also encoded on the magnetic stripe, but not physically embossed or printed on the card. The CVN was added to magnetic stripe cards in the 1990s to reduce counterfeit card fraud resulting from fraudsters using data from paper transaction receipts to create cloned cards. In that era, it was possible to recreate a valid magnetic stripe using just the information embossed on the physical card (or on a printed receipt or a carbon paper copy). The addition of the CVN data element to the magnetic stripe changed this—requiring that the card would have to be read in a magnetic stripe reader to capture all of the data from the magnetic stripe that would be needed to create a counterfeit card. Later, both card network rules and federal legislation required merchants to truncate the card number details from the receipts they provide to their customers—further reducing the potential inadvertent exposure of payment card credentials to fraudsters.

Another fraud control data element, referred to as CVN2, is the three- or four-digit number printed on the signature panel on the back (or, for American Express, on the front) of the card, and used as the "Card Security Code" for card-not-present transactions conducted online. If a merchant captures the CVN2 from the cardholder and forwards it in the authorization message to the issuer, the issuer will respond by indicating its validity—or lack thereof. This helps prevent fraud where a card number is known but where the fraudster hasn't had access to the physical card.

There are a number of other features on the physical cards—some broadly used and some specific to a card brand or card issuer—that have been added over time to help reduce fraud.

Chip Cards

In most countries, cards are migrating from magnetic stripe to chip card (smart card) technology. These cards have both magnetic stripes and chips. In markets where the acceptance infrastructure has been upgraded to support chip reading, counterfeit card fraud should be much more challenging for fraudsters. However, with most cards still usable internationally, including in markets that haven't deployed chip card readers, card fraud often migrates out of the domestic "chip-protected" environment to other countries where only magnetic stripe acceptance still exists. Until a universal chip reading infrastructure exists globally, it's not yet possible for issuers to eliminate reliance on magnetic stripes. Slowly but surely, this migration has gotten underway—but we are likely still several years away from removing the mag stripe from payment cards and relying exclusively on chip technologies. The best that can be done right now is to include an indicator in the magnetic track (in the Service Code field) that tells the terminal it should force a chip read transaction.

Two principal chip standards are used. The first, known as EMV, use an industry standard for a "smart" chip which can perform significant computation within the chip. EMV cards can be recognized by the physical contacts that are present on the face of the card when an EMV chip is present. When inserted into an EMV-capable POS device, contact is made with the card and the chip is powered up to perform processing. EMV cards are most typically implemented in conjunction with PINs, which is referred to as Chip-and-PIN, although in some markets chip cards function in "chip and signature" mode as well. EMV-compliant POS terminals read the EMV cards, validate them, prompt the cardholder to provide a PIN if required, etc.

EMV cards are being introduced on a country-by-country basis as bank issuers and card networks evaluate the costs and benefits associated with their deployment. Many countries, particularly in Europe, made early decisions to migrate to EMV primarily based on concerns about the potential growth in counterfeit card fraud. However, in the U.S. the common assumption was that there wasn't a positive business case to justify a migration to EMV based on the level of counterfeit card fraud on magnetic stripe cards versus the costs associated with upgrading both POS devices and the cards themselves. This changed in August 2011 when Visa introduced rule changes designed to incent merchants to migrate to new POS acceptance devices capable of supporting chip cards by late 2015 (2017 in the case of fuel retailers). Merchants who fail to migrate to new devices become subject to a shift in fraud liability from the issuer—the avoidance of which provides the merchant with the economic incentive to make the upgrade. Unlike in all of the other countries that had migrated to EMV, there was no mandate on U.S. card issuers to issue EMV cards—only the liability shift designed to incent merchant adoption of EMV-capable POS devices.

The second kind of chip standard supports contactless cards. These cards use a simpler, lower-cost chip, based on RFID (radio frequency identification) technology, to pass data between the card and an RFID reader at a POS terminal. Contactless cards were initially implemented primarily as a customer convenience (for speed of checkout), rather than for fraud management—although they do contain technology analogous to the CVN on the magnetic stripe that helps reduce counterfeit fraud at contactless acceptance locations. Contactless acceptance devices are also important to the deployment of certain kinds of mobile payments—particularly those based on the use of near field communication (NFC) technology such as Apple Pay and Android Pay.

Issuers can choose to issue cards containing both EMV and contactless chips. This hybrid approach works well where relatively low value transactions can be performed quickly in contactless mode without requiring a PIN or signature while higher value (presumably more risky) transactions can continue to require full EMV authentication and cardholder verification with PIN or signature at the issuer's option.

POS Acceptance

In the United States, a wide range of point of sale terminal types can read cards and pass the required transaction data on to the acquirer (either to the acquiring bank itself or the bank's processor). These exist both as freestanding devices and as software functionality that is integrated into ECRs (electronic cash registers), mobile tablets or other devices. The acquirer must route the transaction to the correct payment card network; the network then routes the transaction on to the appropriate issuing bank. The figure below shows the extensive interconnection of key nodes in the U.S. market's "payments acceptance grid."

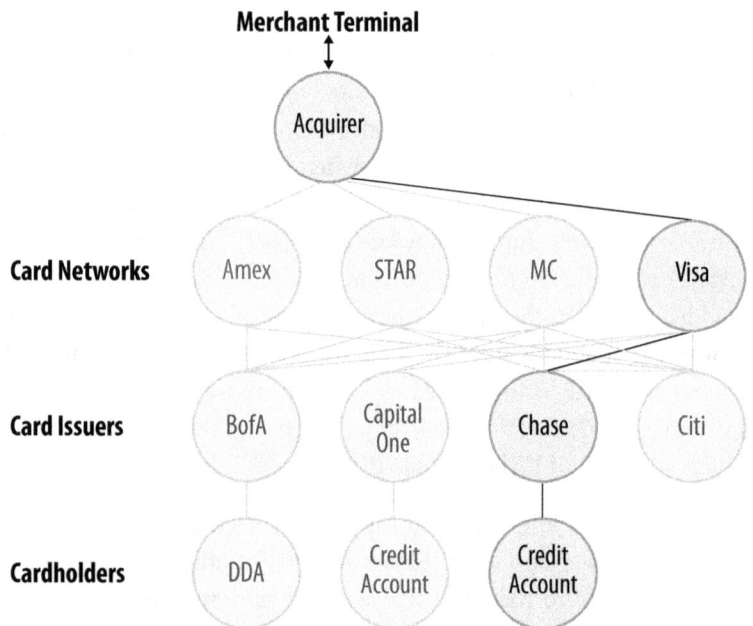

Figure 5-4: The Acceptance Grid

Not all card networks or issuers are shown.

Card Network Processing

Credit card and signature debit transactions (without PINs) are routed through the acceptance grid twice—once in real time for authorization of the transaction and again (typically at the end of the day) for clearing and settlement.

The card network processing hubs sit in the middle, receiving transactions from acquiring member banks (or, more often, from their processors), sorting and switching them to issuing banks and processors. The major card network systems are among the largest online real-time financial systems in the world and, with extensive redundancy and resiliency built in over the years, hold impressive records for ultra-high availability. The architecture of these systems help ensure that high levels of cardholder service can be provided even in the face of various problems with issuer systems, network outages, etc. Stand-in processing can be performed on behalf of issuers at the card network level, for example, to allow transactions to still be processed even when an issuer's systems may be unavailable.

The processing environment is quite different, however, for the two message types:

- The authorization transaction is in real time, with sub-second response times.
- The clearing and settlement transaction occurs in batch, most typically at the end of the day.

PIN debit transactions use a "single message" approach that evolved from their original ATM network heritage. ATM transactions never have subsequent adjustments (such as the addition of a tip to a fine dining purchase), so the single message approach worked well. For PIN debit, the equivalent of an authorization message is sent in real time to the acquirer without a subsequent clearing message. This single message essentially creates its own secondary clearing and settlement message, which is automatically processed—although later and still in batch.

Card Use, Volumes, and Trends

Payment cards are used for many different types of payments. To some extent, these categories define the card products offered by card issuers.

- General-purpose consumer credit, debit, and prepaid cards are used for purchases at merchants and other point of sale locations, for online purchases of goods and services, and to make bill payments.

- Consumer cards are also used for obtaining cash. Debit cards are used for cash withdrawal at ATMs and for "cash back" at certain point of sale locations such as supermarkets. Credit cards may be used for cash advances at either ATMs or bank branches.

- Businesses use business credit and charge cards for travel and entertainment purchases and to make and receive payments from suppliers and customers.

- Both consumers and businesses use cards to make cross-border payments; one of the great strengths of the card payments industry has been its ability to conveniently provide this service to international travelers.

Card Volumes and Growth

Card volume by type looks very different if you look at transaction count vs. transaction amount. Debit transactions exceed credit transactions by count, but are less by amount due to the higher "average ticket" (purchase amount) on credit cards vs. debit cards. Debit cards are typically used for "everyday spend"—lower-value purchases—while credit cards continue to be used for higher-value purchases, travel, entertainment, etc.

Over the last fifteen years, debit card transaction volume has grown much more rapidly than credit. Debit card growth reflects the increasing comfort of consumers with using debit cards for daily purchasing (replacing checks, cash, and, to some extent, credit cards) and, in recent years, for low-value purchases (replacing cash). Widespread merchant acceptance, particularly for signature debit, which can be accepted without PINs, makes debit cards easy and very convenient to use. Some merchants that once accepted checks have also eliminated checks from the tender types they support—further fueling the growth in debit card usage.

Regulation

Law, as well as rules promulgated by regulators and the card networks, controls regulations aimed at protecting consumers. The scope of this regulation at the federal level in the U.S. has been increasing as certain payment card industry practices have come under scrutiny in recent years.

Card Network Operating Rules

The operating rules of open-loop networks—particularly Visa and Master-Card, and to a lesser extent the PIN debit networks—govern most aspects of card issuing, authorization, clearing, and acquiring.

Operating rules are both general (network membership criteria, brand standards, issuance standards, acceptance standards, settlement procedures, arbitration) and specific to card product type and merchant type (as based on merchant category code). Network operating rules also help determine the potential profitability of certain card issuing businesses, because those rules also specify the card network interchange that flows to card issuers for each transaction.

Visa and Mastercard operating rules have historically been very similar. For many years, the common bank owners of the two associations pressured them for "conformance" of their respective rules—as most banks in the U.S. issued both Visa and Mastercard branded cards. With public card company ownership redefining and sharpening the competition between the networks, an increasing number of rules now differ from one network to another. This is particularly problematic for merchants that have to follow these inconsistent rules.

In some cases, primarily related either to fraud or to technologies for which standardization is important, the card companies continue to work together. Examples include jointly-owned organizations such as the PCI Standards Council (PCI-DSS data security requirements for the protection of payment card data) and EMVCo (which owns the standards and intellectual property for EMV chip cards, as well as the standards for EMV-compliant contactless cards, issuer tokenization, and 3D Secure). Typically, Visa, Mastercard, American Express, Discover, JCB and UnionPay are all involved in these organizations.

Card network operating rules may also differ by country and region. Visa and Mastercard have international operating rules that specify treatment of cross-border and interregional transactions. Because cross-border transactions typically involve currency conversion, these kinds of transactions can yield significantly more revenue on a per-transaction basis for both the card issuers (which typically surcharge them to their customers) and the card networks (which handle the currency conversion as part of their settlement function) than do purely domestic transactions. For both Visa and Mastercard, cross-currency transactions provide significant revenue through their management of the currency conversion process.

Changing existing operating rules for an open-loop card network, or creating a new set of rules for a new product, is a complex and time-consuming process. Proposed rules are defined by staff at the card networks and may also be reviewed with some of their client banks. Back in the card association days, multiple committees of member banks (technical, risk management, marketing) may have been involved in reviewing proposed rule changes prior to being formally adopted.

Historically, the board of directors of a card network would give final approval for changed or new rules. Under new public ownership structures today, the management of the card network is responsible for final rules approval. The card networks publish semiannual calendars of upcoming rule changes, giving client banks and their processors time for any system or policy changes needed to implement each new rule. The card networks have been criticized for the accumulated complexity of their operating rules—and recently have undertaken efforts to simplify them where possible. Under the new public ownership structures, the card networks' operating rules have been made publicly available and can be inspected by regulators, potential customers, and other interested parties.

> **Network Competition**
>
> Keep in mind that card networks compete with each other for payments volume. Rule changes can make it possible for a card network to compete in a new market segment. For example, some PIN debit networks approved rule changes to allow PIN-less debit bill payment. The basic rules of the PIN debit networks require the entry of a PIN into a hardware-encrypted device. This rule effectively shut the PIN debit networks out of the eCommerce domain, and prohibited billers from routing Internet-initiated debit card bill payments through the lower-cost PIN debit networks. The rule change simply removed the PIN entry requirement for certain categories of billers—a segmentation strategy based upon billers not likely to be paid fraudulently. Voilà—the PIN debit networks can now compete for that volume.

Closed loop networks, such as American Express, have card issuance policies similar to some provisions of the open-loop card network rules, so as to ensure interoperability for merchants and other users of the payments system. Merchant agreements, for similar reasons, are much like those of open-loop card networks. But a closed loop network is free to change such policies and agreements without the involved processes used by open-loop networks.

Federal Legislation

The Federal Truth in Lending Act of 1968 resulted in Federal Reserve Bank Regulation Z taking effect the following year. The Act and Regulation Z were aimed at protecting borrowing consumers by requiring full and clear disclosure of terms and rates. Provisions in Regulation Z were strengthened and clarified in 1988 when the Fair Credit and Charge Card Disclosure Act was enacted.

The Electronic Fund Transfer Act, which took effect in 1980, was implemented by Reg E for debit cards. This act was also amended in 2009 to cover gift cards.

In 2009, Congress approved the Credit Card Accountability Responsibility and Disclosure Act of 2009, which significantly increased federal regulation of certain aspects of credit card issuance. Again aimed at consumer protection, the Act specifies detailed requirements on interest rate setting, billing practices, and certain notifications to consumers. The Act stopped short of specifying fees or rate caps.

In 2010, Congress approved the Dodd-Frank Act—perhaps the most significant piece of financial reform legislation in recent history. The so-called

Durbin Amendment regulating debit card interchange and network routing was included in this legislation as was the creation of the new Consumer Financial Protection Bureau (CFPB) which consolidates most Federal consumer financial protection authority in one place. The bureau's activities related to credit cards has included building a database of credit card agreements from more than 300 card issuers, conducting and reporting on a semiannual survey of the terms of credit card plans offered by financial institutions, and examining credit card marketing agreements with universities, colleges, or affiliated organizations such as alumni associations, sororities, fraternities, and foundations. Every two years, the CFPB reports on the state of the consumer credit card market that covers how consumers use cards, the price they pay for using them, the availability of credit cards, the practices used by credit card companies, and innovation.

Network Economics and Interchange

In the sections that follow, we will discuss the business models for card issuance and card acquiring. But first, we'll discuss the card networks themselves as they are also now no longer bank-owned associations but real, publicly traded companies—with their own economic models and public shareholders.

The Network Business

Running an open-loop card network involves functions such as these:

- Transaction switching among banks participating in the network

- Net settlement among banks, usually on a daily basis and including multi-currency settlement

- Creation, updating, maintenance, and enforcement of operating rules, including setting interchange fees

- Management of network membership, including defining and enforcing criteria (such as financial strength) for membership

- Creation and maintenance of brands and brand promotion strategies

- Arbitration of disputes between network participants

Most networks also provide additional services to network participants. These may include additional processing services, including risk management, and a variety of information products. The network operating rules may mandate that participants use some services; others are optional.

The revenue models for the card networks consist of processing fees and brand-use service fees assessed on all transactions made with a card carrying the network brand. As they compete for the loyalty of card issuers to their brands, the card networks may offer larger issuers incentives in terms of additional services or reductions in assessments in exchange for issuer commitments to issue their network-branded cards. For a card network, obtaining issuance is fundamentally important—the network's business begins with having cards issued that include their brand.

The global card networks also earn significant revenue from handling the foreign exchange aspects of all cross-currency transactions. A cross-currency transaction—with its "built-in" foreign exchange revenue opportunity—can be substantially more profitable to the card networks than domestic transactions where no currency conversion is required.

Offsetting a network's revenues are the costs of operating substantial transaction processing centers; a global telecommunications infrastructure; staff required to handle the rules and perform product management and member relations functions; and the expenses associated with brand promotion and advertising.

Perhaps the most unusual—and interesting—aspect of the card industry is the networks' role in card interchange fees. The networks set the interchange rates, but, as we will see, do not directly participate in the financial flow associated with interchange fees, nor do they receive any revenue from them.

Interchange is, however, a critical element of a card network's business model. Since the card network's issuing customers are the recipients of interchange fees, the level of interchange that a network sets is an important element in the network's competitive position. A higher level of interchange on one network's card products naturally makes that network's card products more financially attractive to card issuers. In a market in which issuers are free to choose to issue card products from among multiple networks, interchange fee income becomes an important criterion in the decision made by an issuer as to which card brand and card products to issue.

Card Network Interchange

Interchange is a feature of open-loop card networks that was originally introduced to bring into balance the costs borne by the card issuer and merchant acquirer to provide the card payment service.

The rationale for the unusual economic structure of interchange rests on the concept that one "side" of the transaction, the merchant (and its acquiring bank), benefits from the use of the card (primarily through increased merchant sales), while the other "side," the card issuer, incurs costs associated with making this use possible. Interchange is the mechanism the card networks established early on to have the value-receiving merchant compensate the cost-incurring issuer for some of the issuer's expenses. It would be too complex, according to this rationale, to have each issuer individually negotiate compensation with each merchant. The network, by defining the appropriate cost reimbursement between the parties, defines how the economics work.

In establishing the original framework for interchange, the card networks utilized third-party accounting firms to study issuer, acquirer, and merchant costs and to recommend a fee structure that would ensure a balanced approach was the result: what one network termed IRF, an "issuer reimbursement fee." The framework used for this examination put costs into three categories:

- **Cost of guarantee.** The card issuer is extending a payment guarantee to the merchant—the merchant is paid even if the cardholder subsequently fails to pay the card issuer what he or she owes.

- **Cost of funds.** The merchant receives payment from the issuing bank (via the card network) before the issuing bank is paid by the cardholder.

- **Operating expenses.** The issuing bank has expenses in operating its authorization network, producing statements, handling customer service, etc.

Because much of the costs of providing the card payment service are borne by issuers, interchange fees provided the mechanism for issuers to be compensated for a portion of those costs by assessing acquirers who, ultimately, pass the costs on to their merchant customers.

Each card transaction involves two banks with interchange being a fee that one bank pays to the other as compensation for some of its costs. The network sets the interchange fee and determines the direction of payment (which bank pays the other). In the United States, interchange flows from the acquiring bank to the issuing bank on purchase transactions. As such, interchange is an expense to the acquiring bank and revenue to the card issuing bank. (Note that interchange on ATM transactions flows in reverse—the card issuer pays an interchange fee to the ATM deployer for servicing the issuer's cardholder.)

The merchant's acquiring bank, of course, passes this interchange expense along to its customer, the merchant. The acquiring bank's fee to the merchant is known as the "merchant discount fee," of which interchange is the largest single component. While interchange is often equated with the merchant discount fee, it's not the same thing—just the largest component. This is illustrated below.

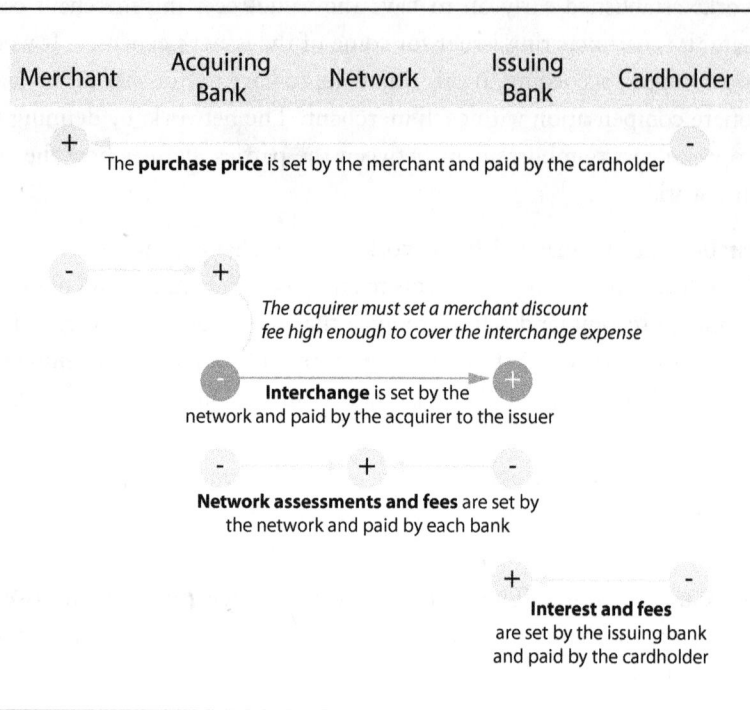

Merchant	Acquiring Bank	Network	Issuing Bank	Cardholder

+   -

The **purchase price** is set by the merchant and paid by the cardholder

-      +

The acquirer must set a merchant discount fee high enough to cover the interchange expense

-      +

Interchange is set by the network and paid by the acquirer to the issuer

-      +   -

Network assessments and fees are set by the network and paid by each bank

+   -

Interest and fees are set by the issuing bank and paid by the cardholder

Figure 5-5: Card Network Interchange

Acquirers typically quote prices to larger merchants based on "interchange plus" pricing—meaning that interchange fees (along with card network assessments and transaction fees that the acquirers must also pay to the networks) are passed through to the merchant—with the acquirer's additional fees priced on top of those. With this so-called "interchange plus" approach, acquirers are insulated from changes to interchange fees—they simply pass them through to the merchants, including any adjustments the card networks may make to the fees over time. Merchants also like the transparency that this approach provides, as they get to see the major expenses that the acquirer incurs.

Smaller merchants are typically quoted a blended rate for their merchant discount fee and may not have visibility to the underlying interchange and assessment components of the merchant discount fee. Many small merchants lack the sophistication to be concerned about that level of detail but, as merchants become more successful and handle higher volumes of payments, they will likely begin to pay attention and may want to move to an "interchange plus" pricing arrangement with their acquirer.

Interchange fees also vary based on the card product type used by the consumer and the merchant handling of the transaction. Interchange fees are calculated and applied by the card networks, literally, on a transaction-by-transaction level.

	Mastercard & Visa Credit Card	American Express Card	Regulated Debit Card	Exempt Debit Card
Note: all rates are illustrative only, and meant to describe the relative levels of interchange (on open-loop networks) and the resulting merchant discount fee for a $100 purchase. The acquiring markup will vary considerably based on the size of the merchant. "Regulated" and "Exempt" refer to Fed Reg II, discussed below.				
Interchange	$1.75	N/A	$0.25	$0.51
Acquiring Markup	$0.15	N/A	$0.10	$0.10
Total Merchant Discount Fee	$2.00	$2.50	$0.34	$0.61

Table 5-4: Comparative Interchange

The Evolution of Interchange

Although each card network originally had only one interchange rate, the networks, over time, realized that setting different rates to accomplish certain objectives was an effective segmentation strategy to help expand card acceptance to new merchant categories.

The first major incentive interchange rate was introduced in the 1980s, when the networks established a lower interchange rate for transactions handled by electronic draft capture POS terminals in lieu of paper sales drafts. This lower incentive interchange rate provided the primary economic rationale for merchants to migrate from paper-based to electronic draft capture POS terminals. Over the course of several years in the late 1980's, almost all of the merchants in the U.S. completed this migration—saving on interchange fees, but also improving the ease and convenience of paying by card.

Since then, many additional interchange rates have been defined, for particular merchant categories (for example, a low interchange rate was introduced to provide an incentive for grocery stores to begin accepting credit cards), certain types of transactions (eCommerce, bill payment), and certain types of cards (small business, premium rewards cards, etc.). Over the years, the complexity of the interchange schedules of the card networks has grown—for example, Mastercard's interchange schedule is over 100 pages long.

The interchange rate a merchant pays on a particular transaction is determined by the combination of all such factors. Not surprisingly, given this segmented approach, cost today does not appear to be the sole factor in determining card network interchange.

Interchange rates also vary by payments system. Signature debit card interchange is lower than credit card interchange, and PIN debit interchange is even lower for unregulated debit card issuers. Larger debit card issuers (with over $10 billion in assets) receive regulated interchange rates that do not distinguish between signature or PIN debit usage.

Closed loop networks do not have interchange, although the network assesses to the merchant a "merchant discount fee" which is generally similar to the merchant discount fee that an acquiring bank charges for a merchant's access to the open-loop networks. In a closed loop network, the entire discount fee is kept by the network rather than being shared among three parties (acquiring bank, network, and issuing bank). As the traditional closed loop networks—American Express and Discover—have recently been opening up to working with acquirers to expand acceptance of their card brands, they have created an analogous structure which provides compensation to acquirers for their help in increasing acceptance.

In Australia, the EU, and some other countries, bank regulatory and competition authorities have stepped in and mandated reductions in interchange rates. In the U.S., interchange rates have been repeatedly, but unsuccessfully, challenged in court by merchants seeking to have them reduced.

The Interchange Controversy

Interchange has been controversial, in both the United States and other markets. Although the arguments are complex, the two general points of view can be summarized as follows:

Perspective One: Interchange is an economic structure necessary to enable a global network of great benefit to all participants; it is the most effective way of managing what economists refer to as a "two-sided market."

Perspective Two: Interchange is a form of price fixing that unfairly constrains merchants' ability to directly negotiate prices for a key service (card acceptance).

A middle ground holds that the mechanism is effective, but needs some form of governmental control to ensure that interchange rates remain reasonable. This group notes that network competition for issuance leads to rising, rather than falling, prices. This occurs because the network's customer (the issuing bank, which decides which network to use) receives the price that the network sets. In a "normal" market, a customer pays the price their provider sets.

One concept that has growing appeal among some groups is to not regulate interchange, but instead prohibit card network rules that ban surcharges. This would allow merchants to charge consumers an additional fee for acceptance of high-interchange cards, for example. This has worked in some markets (e.g., Australia), but has proven impractical in the U.S. due to state laws in many states that prohibit merchants from surcharging customers.

Over the years, various merchant coalitions have lobbied regulators and legislators in the U.S. for "interchange relief." To the banking industry's apparent surprise, the 2010 Dodd-Frank financial reform bill contained a provision—known as the "Durbin Amendment"—that gave the Fed the responsibility to determine appropriate debit card interchange rates.

In 2011, the Fed fulfilled its new responsibilities under this legislation and published Regulation II that set interchange fees on debit cards for "regulated" bank issuers—those with over $100 billion in assets—as well as required that all debit card issuers provide two unaffiliated debit networks on their cards with merchants being able to choose which network would route the transaction on a transaction-by-transaction basis.

Litigation between merchants and the card companies has continued to evolve with new cases that continue to argue for various forms of relief. As with other jurisdictions around the world, interchange remains an important area of focus for merchants in the U.S. seeking to reduce payments acceptance costs.

Card Issuance—Credit and Charge Cards

The credit card has been called "the most profitable product in banking history" in the United States and the credit card market is one of the largest consumer markets in the nation. With industry revenues estimated at well over $100 billion annually and revolving credit card balances exceeding $925 billion, it is clearly a very attractive business.

In addition to its substantial revenues, three factors characterize the credit card issuance industry in the United States—factors that do not apply in many other countries.

> **Credit Concentration**
>
> Within the large credit card issuing banks, the organization responsible for credit card issuance is a separate business unit, removed from the retail bank organization that manages consumer checking accounts and issues debit cards. As a result, it's quite typical that a bank other than the one holding the consumer's checking account has issued a consumer's primary credit card.

- **Near-universal acceptance.** Almost all retail establishments in the U.S. accept credit cards, as do many non-retail enterprises, including billers, manufacturers, distributors and wholesalers, governments, non-profits, and educational institutions.

- **A saturated marketplace.** The CFPB reports that most adult Americans—about 63%—have an open credit card. Many Americans without access to credit have debit or prepaid cards.

- **Multiple cards.** Of Americans who have a credit card, most have nearly four credit cards each. They are used to choosing between those cards at the point of sale based on a wide variety of factors, including available credit lines, rewards, and purpose of the purchase.

These factors have contributed to a sharp increase in the concentration of the credit card issuing marketplace in the United States. The top ten U.S. credit card issuers handled over 80% of total general-purpose card purchase volume at the end of 2015—including (in the top 5) JP Morgan Chase, Bank of America, Citibank, Capital One and Wells Fargo.

What Credit Card Issuers Do

- **Determine card offerings.** Issuers choose which networks to use, which types of network-branded cards to offer, and which issuer-specific customizations to offer. Major issuers often have hundreds of product variations available. Determining the type and level of rewards offered on a card is an important part of this task. Some baseline card rewards levels are dictated by card network product standards; the issuer customizes others.

- **Solicit new cardholders.** Through mailings, "take-ones," online sites, bank branches, and onsite event leads. Co-branded and affinity cards are a way for some issuers to find new customers at a reasonable cost by partnering with merchants or member associations. Credit underwriting and fraud scoring must be done before approving a new cardholder.

- **Issue cards.** Card issuers must physically issue cards to cardholders, personalized with data on magnetic stripe and chips, and manage card activation (preventing fraud from cards lost in the mail).

- **Compete for purchase volume and balances.** Card issuers strive for "top of wallet" positioning—for both POS and online purchases. (Online, a "card on file" at an eCommerce merchant or travel site equals a virtual "top of wallet").

- **Manage credit and fraud exposures.** The U.S. credit bureaus provide sophisticated tools, which issuers supplement with internal systems, to manage ongoing credit exposure. Other tools, provided by third parties or developed internally, help manage transaction fraud—often dynamically (prior to transaction authorization).

- **Manage operations, including authorization, clearing, statementing, and customer service.** Part of this is responding to customer and merchant inquiries and handling disputes—including the so-called "chargeback."

- **Manage the cost of funds.** Issuers also manage the sale of securities to fund additional receivables.

- **Manage collections.** Issuers attempt to collect bad debt from consumers who don't pay off their debts. Issuers often sell bad debt to third-party collectors.

What is a Chargeback? (Part 1)

A chargeback is a card industry term referring to a set of rules that spell out issuer, acquirer, and merchant responsibilities in the event of a disputed transaction. The rules give issuers the right to reverse a credit to the merchant's account (to "charge it back") under certain circumstances based on a series of "chargeback codes" with associated rules and rights.

There are three broad types of disputes and corresponding types of chargebacks. A "fraud" chargeback is initiated when the consumer claims they don't recognize the purchase or didn't authorize the transaction. This is sometimes referred to as the I-didn't-do-it chargeback. A "service" chargeback is initiated when the consumer has not received the goods or service as promised and the merchant refuses or is unable to make the consumer whole. A "technical" chargeback is initiated to correct a technical billing mistake. The consumer recognizes the purchase, is satisfied with the goods, but didn't agree to be charged five times for the same purchase!

Credit Card Processors

Issuing processors may do some or all of the tasks listed above. A very small bank might entirely outsource its card program to an issuer processor handling all activity, including taking and managing credit exposure, with the bank simply putting its brand on the product. A larger bank may outsource authorization and clearing, but handle all other tasks in-house; some of the very largest issuers chose to perform essentially all functions in-house.

The two largest processors in the U.S. for credit card processing are First Data Corp. and TSYS. In addition to credit card processing, they also providing processing services for debit and prepaid cards along with merchant acquiring.

In addition to the card processors, issuers may also rely on other companies to assist in various business areas. These companies:

- Assist issuers in using a wide variety of consumer databases to help target potentially profitable consumers for solicitation and for other marketing programs.

- Provide issuers with card plastic production, independent of the processor or in-house production department.

- Help issuers with products that assist in predicting credit defaults, adjusting credit lines, and attempting to maximize portfolio profitability.

- Support issuers who choose to outsource collections to third parties and who may, ultimately, sell the debt for a small fraction of its value to a third-party debt buyer that pursues debt collections independently of the original issuer.

Credit and Charge Card Products

- **Charge cards** have no revolving credit associated with them and require the cardholder to pay the balance in full each month.

- **Revolving credit cards** are the basic credit card we all know so well: the cardholder is given the option to pay the balance in full each month (becoming, in industry parlance, a "transactor") or to make partial payments over a period of time (becoming a "revolver"). Most consumer credit cards provide a "grace period" that allows the cardholder to avoid paying interest on purchases as long as the balance is paid in full. As a result, transactors almost never pay interest charges. Revolvers, on the other hand, carry a balance from month to month and pay interest charges based upon the amount of credit extended. Revolvers also generally are charged interest from the date of purchase.

- **Premium cards,** in gold and platinum and more, are defined by the card network and may offer a variety of special services as well as enhanced rewards.

- **Affinity and co-branded cards.** Affinity cards carry the name and brand of an organization (perhaps a school, alumni association, or football team). Co-branded cards are a joint product offering of the sponsor and the issuing bank. Terms of these deals vary, but generally the sponsor gets some financial benefits (particularly on purchases made at the sponsor's outlets) and the issuer gets a lower-cost source of new customers. Both issuers and networks are typically involved in the competition for a new co-brand relationship.

- **Small business cards**. Revolving credit or charge cards offered to small businesses, often with specialized rewards programs.

- **Corporate cards.** Charge cards issued to the employees of a corporation, to be used primarily for travel and entertainment purchases.

- **Purchasing cards.** Charge cards issued to a corporation (to either employees or departments), used to buy goods and services from company suppliers.

- **Private label cards.** Closed loop cards offered by a single sponsor; most common are gasoline and department store cards. Private label cards are not usable at other merchants. Typically, a merchant contracts with a large issuing bank to do the work and take some or all of the credit exposure.

Credit and Charge Card Economics

The economics of the credit card industry are dominated by interest earned on revolving loans to credit cardholders who are revolvers. The interchange component of the merchant discount fee in an open-loop network, and the entire merchant discount fee in a closed loop network, are important, but secondary, sources of revenue. Charge cards, without the interest income from consumer borrowing, must rely exclusively on interchange and cardholder fees for revenue.

Offsetting revenue are credit losses, cost of funds, fraud losses and operating expenses. The costs of soliciting new cardholders and providing rewards programs both to attract new cardholders and to compete for "top of wallet" position on spending are also considerable.

The credit card issuing business can be very profitable. The figure below shows a typical large credit card issuer's P&L—in "normal" economic times. Note credit losses are shown here as a percent of revenue. More typically, the industry looks at losses as a percent of outstanding receivables. That loss rate is usually around 5%—but in times of recession can climb to 10% or more—resulting in losses for the issuer during those years.

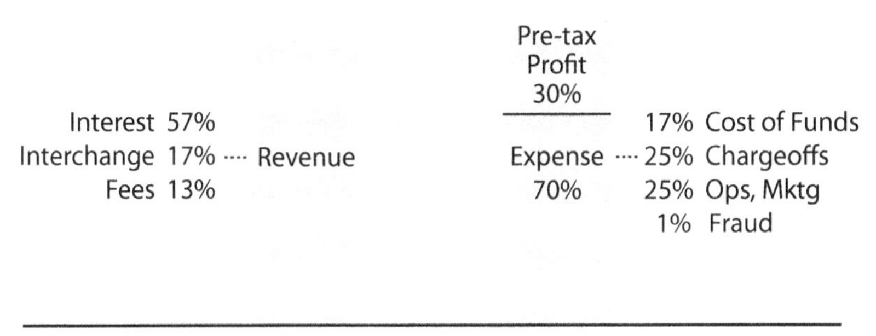

		Pre-tax Profit 30%		
Interest 57%			17%	Cost of Funds
Interchange 17% ···· Revenue		Expense ····	25%	Chargeoffs
Fees 13%		70%	25%	Ops, Mktg
			1%	Fraud

Figure 5-6: Typical Credit Card Issuer P&L

Credit Card Issuance Strategy

Bank strategies regarding credit vary considerably. Some banks take an aggressive posture, lending to riskier borrowers and compensating with aggressive credit line management and collection policies. Others are more conservative—perhaps choosing to only extend credit cards to existing customers of the bank and not the broader population.

Similarly, banks vary in terms of their marketing strategies: some market credit cards only to existing customers who have banking (checking account) relationships with them; others aggressively court new customers anywhere they may live. All banks, of course, are vulnerable to credit cycles in the economy and to how those cycles may affect consumers' ability to repay debt.

> ### Rewards Programs
>
> The cost of developing and administering rewards programs is increasingly important to the credit card industry. The CFPB reports that, as of 2014, accounts with rewards programs represent nearly two-thirds of all credit card balances and four-fifths of all credit card spending.

Card issuers are becoming more active in their management of credit and charge card interchange revenue. From a credit card issuer's standpoint, the level of interchange income received is based primarily upon the type of card issued. American Express (which now can be issued by other banks following the outcome of earlier litigation against Visa and Mastercard), Visa Signature, and Mastercard WorldCard products are higher interchange products, as are small business cards. To increase interchange revenue, issuers have migrated some existing cards to these products as they go through reissuance, as well as using them and their higher rewards features to try to gain new customers. The costs of network-mandated rewards programs and other network-defined product features can offset some of the increased interchange revenue.

Annual card fees, once a common feature of the card industry, have significantly declined in importance; competition has mostly reduced or eliminated annual fees for traditional credit cards. Punitive fees for over-limit or late payments are also important elements of issuer revenue.

Card Issuance—Debit Cards

A debit card enables a customer to make a purchase by using funds from the balance available in a checking account. As shown below, a debit card can be thought of as a hybrid of a credit card and a check; it has some similarities to both, but with the source of funds remaining in the checking account.

Attribute	Credit Card	Debit Card	Check
Type	Electronic, "pull"	Electronic, "pull"	Paper, "pull"
Source of Funds	Credit	Checking account	Checking account
Risk to Merchant	Guaranteed	Guaranteed	Not guaranteed
Economics for Issuing (Consumer) Bank	Loan interest, interchange, fees	Net interest income, interchange, fees	Net interest income, fees

Table 5-5: Debit Card Comparisons

Signature and PIN Debit

In the U.S., there are two primary types of debit transactions: signature debit, routed through the Visa or Mastercard networks ("riding the credit card rails") and PIN debit, routed through one or more of the ATM or PIN debit networks. The physical debit card used for either of these transactions is the same, with the same PAN (primary account number) used regardless of the transaction routing. As mentioned earlier, the evolution of the credit card networks paralleled the evolution of the debit card networks; eventually they came together when Visa and Mastercard launched their signature debit card products.

The routing of the transaction, however, has meaningful differences in terms of the rules and interchange fees that apply to it.

The routing decision is actually made by a combination of consumer choice and merchant choice at the point of acceptance, and depends on several factors:

- If the merchant does not have a PIN pad, the transaction is always routed through the signature networks. The PIN debit networks require PIN entry at the physical point of sale.

- If the merchant does have a PIN pad, the merchant's system may look up the PAN (using information provided by the merchant's acquirer) and determine that the card transaction can be routed to a PIN debit network. If so, the merchant POS in real time may prompt the consumer for PIN entry, thereby "steering" the transaction through the lower-cost PIN networks, unless the consumer is aware of the difference and asks that the transaction be routed through the "credit" networks (by cancelling the request for PIN at the POS). Note that the Durbin Amendment and the resulting Federal Reserve Regulation II eliminated any potential differential in cost between signature and PIN debit for regulated debit card issuers.

- Some merchants do not steer, but leave the choice up to the consumer.

- In card-not-present transactions, routing is almost always classified as signature debit. However, in recent years, the PIN debit networks have been allowing some low-risk transactions, such as online bill payment, to flow through their networks without a PIN—the so-called "PINless debit" acceptance category. Several startup companies are also attempting to bring PIN debit transactions to eCommerce merchants.

- With the passage of the Dodd-Frank Act in 2010 with the so-called Durbin Amendment, the Federal Reserve was given responsibility to set new rules with respect to routing of debit card transactions. These new routing rules apply to all debit cards, not just to debit cards issued by "regulated issuers" with over $10 billion in assets. In general, the new Regulation II debit routing rules require that issuers equip their cards so they can be routed over at least two unaffiliated debit networks—and provide that the merchants shall have the ability to make the choice as to how to route on a transaction-by-transaction basis.

As shown in the table below, the differences between signature and PIN debit primarily relate to the authentication used and the routing/processing of the transaction. As overall debit purchases continue to grow, bank debit card issuer focus appears to be switching away from a "war between PIN and signature" and simply to more support for debit in general as the best alternative to consumer use of checks.

Attribute	Signature Debit	PIN Debit
Type	Pull payment	Pull payment
Authentication	Signature	PIN
Merchant Guaranty	Full (Card-present)	Full (Card-present)
Processing	Dual message	Single message
Network Interchange	Regulated for large banks	Regulated for large banks

Table 5-6: Signature and PIN Debit

Debit Volumes

Over the last fifteen years, debit card volumes have grown rapidly in the U.S. market and now account for more consumer purchase transactions and more spending, on an annual basis, than either credit cards or checks. Debit card growth has come as debit cards have replaced:

- **Checks.** Consumers find debit cards more convenient than checks at the point of sale and many merchants have found it more acceptable to simply not accept checks. Many consumers also use their debit card to directly pay billers online.

- **Credit cards.** Some "convenience" users of credit cards, who routinely pay off their monthly balance, have switched to debit cards. Others continue to use credit cards, primarily to get the higher rewards available on credit cards.

- **Cash.** A more recent trend has been the use of debit cards for very small transactions—particularly now that, at many merchants, a signature on the receipt is not required for such transactions.

> ### KYC
>
> In order to open a checking account for a customer and issue a debit card, a bank must go through a "Know Your Customer" process mandated by the USA PATRIOT Act of 2001. Though this is not generally thought of as a debit card function, a bank can't issue a debit card if it hasn't completed this process.

Debit Card Economics

For the consumer's bank, the debit card is not a product in the same sense that a credit card is. A debit card is a component—now, a very important component—of the checking account product. This is true both for consumer and small business checking accounts. Unlike with credit cards—where a consumer might choose to have several cards from different issuers—only one debit card from their primary relationship bank is typically in the consumer's wallet.

Although some revenues, and some expenses, can be attributed directly to the debit card, the consumer does not make a buying decision to acquire a debit card. Rather, the consumer chooses a bank for their checking account, and is then automatically issued a debit card (which, of course, is also an ATM card).

A retail bank P&L might look something like the example shown in the table below. Note that there is little direct relationship between sources of revenue and categories of expense.

Sources of Revenue
Net interest income: value of balances in checking account
Interchange from debit card transactions
Routine monthly fees
Exceptional fees (overdraft, etc.)

Categories of Expense
Branches, customer service centers
Systems: transaction processing, networks, statements, online and mobile banks, online bill payment, etc.
Risk management
Marketing and rewards programs

Table 5-7: Debit Card Issuer P&L

It is clear, however, that increasing the use of debit cards, particularly as they displace check and cash transactions, will grow revenue at a bank. This is simply because the bank earns interchange revenue on every debit card transaction, but nothing on cash or checks (except in the case of non-sufficient funds). Banks, therefore, spend time and attention on debit card activation, the industry term used for getting a consumer to start using the debit card—not just for ATM access but also for everyday purchases. Note that the Durbin Amendment and the resulting Federal Reserve Regulation II has significantly reduced interchange fee revenue for regulated debit card issuers.

Bouncing Cards?

In the early days of debit cards, many banks were wary that debit cards might reduce the NSF ("bounced check") fees from the checking business. Since a debit card was authorized and, therefore, couldn't bounce, the thinking went, banks stood to lose a lot of the money they were then earning from bounced check fees. After a few years, some smart bankers figured out that they could actually go ahead and authorize debit transactions against insufficient balances, and charge the cardholder an overdraft fee, thereby replicating the NSF income stream. This was so successful that banks increased both the rate and frequency of these charges. This led to a significant consumer backlash against the "$35 overdraft fee on a $5 cup of coffee," leading the Federal Reserve Bank to impose new regulations requiring banks to have consumers "opt in" for overdraft protection.

What the Debit Card Issuer Does

- Issue cards to cardholders, personalized with data on magnetic stripe and (for some cards) contactless chips; manage card activation.

- Choose and manage the ATM and debit card networks, managing the expense of network fees against the interchange revenue (for debit cards) and revenue or expense (for ATMs) offered by the network.

- Manage fraud.

- Manage overdraft and collections on overdrafts extended.

- Manage operations, including authorization and clearing. Note that many operational tasks, including statement production and customer service, are done for the checking account product as a whole, and not specifically for debit cards.

- Define and manage debit card rewards programs. Generally, debit card rewards are less "rich" than credit card rewards, because of the lesser interchange revenue from debit card transactions, which funds the costs of rewards. With the reduction in interchange revenue post-Regulation II, debit card rewards programs have

Checking Debit Card Transactions

Debit card authorization is more challenging than credit card authorization, as the bank must check against an ever-changing account balance. In the early days of debit, banks would authorize transactions (or have a processor authorize them) against a "shadow file" that could be hours or even days out of date. Now, however, most large banks handle authorizations dynamically against the "real" balance in the checking account.

mostly disappeared for regulated debit card issuers but are still sometimes provided by exempt debit card issuers.

Debit Card Issuer Processors

As with credit cards, debit card processors provide debit card issuers with outsourced processing services for their debit card programs as an alternative to in-house processing. Major providers include Visa DPS, First Data Corp., TSYS, Vantiv, Mastercard Payment Transaction Services, FIS, Fiserv, and others.

Debit Card Competition

Banks' share of the debit card market naturally tracks the distribution of checking accounts. As the U.S. is not a concentrated retail banking market, debit card issuers are much less concentrated than credit card issuers. Also, a consumer may have multiple credit cards, but typically only one debit card. In general, debit card issuance follows a retail bank's checking account market share.

There is, however, competition in the debit brand and network areas—and it is a bit more complex than that for credit cards. Competition exists between the signature debit and PIN debit networks (discussed above), and among brands within signature and PIN debit. Visa and Mastercard compete for signature debit volume, but also own PIN debit networks (in the case of Visa, one of the major ones). There are multiple PIN debit networks, many operating on a local or regional basis. The national PIN debit networks (STAR, NYCE, and Accel/Exchange) are owned by major bank processors. Competition for debit issuance and merchant routing of debit card transactions has intensified since the Federal Reserve has imposed its new Regulation II debit rules on the industry.

Debit Card Issuing Banks	PIN Debit Networks
Bank of America	Interlink (Visa)
Wells Fargo	Maestro (Mastercard)
JPMorgan Chase	STAR (First Data Corp.)
All other banks and credit unions	NYCE (FIS)
Signature Debit Networks	Accel (Fiserv)
Visa	Pulse (Discover)
Mastercard	and others
Not all providers or all categories are shown	

Table 5-8: Major Providers—Debit Card Issuance

Debit Card Rewards

Some banks may provide consumers with rewards for debit card usage. This makes sense for "non-regulated" debit issuing banks, which want consumers to "activate"—and many consumers have come to expect card rewards.

The challenge to debit issuers is financial: there isn't a lot of interchange revenue on debit cards—especially those of regulated debit issuers—to fund the cost of providing rewards. So consumers, used to high reward levels on most of their credit cards, are often disappointed with the relatively low levels of rewards on debit cards. Banks are using a variety of strategies to create rewards programs that satisfy both their desire for debit card activation and consumer expectations:

- Relationship rewards. These programs provide consumers with rewards points for a variety of checking account actions; there may be different points awarded for PIN and signature debit, for using the bank's electronic bill payment service, for receipt of an electronic statement, etc.

- Merchant-funded rewards. These programs provide richer rewards when a customer shops at one of a set of merchants in the bank's rewards network. The merchants fund the rewards. Typically, these networks are "category-exclusive"—they have only one merchant per category (e.g., hardware store or coffee shop).

> **The Debit Card Brand Decision**
>
> When the card networks introduced signature debit to banks, they didn't permit dual issuance of debit cards—meaning that a bank that issued a Visa signature debit card could not also issue a Mastercard signature debit card. Helped by this policy, Visa took an early lead in debit brand share. Visa's strategy of providing complete debit card processing (card issuance, authorization, and clearing) for banks also helped win bank issuance decisions.

New Types of Debit Cards

Although most debit cards in the U.S. use either the signature or PIN debit networks to access funds in a consumer's checking account, it is possible to use the ACH network to accomplish nearly the same thing. A bank (or a non-bank service provider) can provide a consumer with a card (or a non-card token) that, when presented and authenticated, triggers an ACH debit transaction and pulls funds for the purchase from the consumer's checking account.

Some department stores or gas companies use this technique today. A single-purpose card is given to the consumer, who presents it at purchase; an ACH transaction is triggered. The merchant saves by paying no merchant discount fee, but bears NSF risk. Some grocery stores are "payment-enabling" their loyalty cards in this fashion. While these single-purpose cards look like a traditional debit card, they are actually ACH POS cards and are governed by NACHA rules.

Another variation is referred to as a "decoupled" debit card. A "normal" signature debit card is issued to a consumer by a bank different from the one at which the consumer has a checking account. The issuer authorizes the merchant transaction through normal card authorization processing, and then uses ACH to pull funds from the consumer's checking account—which the consumer registered upon enrollment. The issuer keeps the signature debit interchange, but bears the risk of NSF or fraud on the ACH transaction.

Debit or Credit?

At Glenbrook's Payments Boot Camps, one of the most frequent questions we get is, "Why do people use debit cards instead of credit cards?" Our Boot Camp attendees, of course, are payments professionals—relatively affluent business people. Almost without exception, they use credit cards, not debit cards, for their "everyday spend," and enjoy the rewards that come with this. Many of these people don't carry credit card balances—they are "transactors" in card industry parlance. They don't understand why someone would choose to use a debit card. They think of their credit card as a debit card with rewards.

There are several answers to this question. Some consumers have been "burned" by credit card usage, and avoid credit cards in order to avoid incurring debt and interest and fees related to this. Others have a philosophical or moral objection to the use of credit, and avoid credit cards even if paid off every month.

But we think the best answer is that most people aren't asking themselves the question, "Should I use a credit or a debit card?" Instead, they want to spend the money they have in their bank account, and are asking the question, "How should I do this?" They can withdraw cash from their account, and pay that way; they can write a check on the account, or they can use their debit card. The debit card, for many people, wins on convenience and ease of use.

Card Issuance—Prepaid Cards

Prepaid cards are a special type of debit card. Purchases made with a prepaid card draw on funds already in an account—not upon a line of credit. But rather than drawing on funds kept in the cardholder's checking account, a prepaid card draws on a different type of account, kept on behalf of the cardholder by the issuer of the card.

There are two types of prepaid cards: closed loop and open-loop cards. Closed loop cards are usable only at the sponsor's store or stores. Open-loop cards carry a network brand and are usable anywhere that network's brand is accepted.

In the U.S. market, closed loop cards account for roughly three quarters of the prepaid card "load" (value) each year, but the open-loop network-branded cards are growing much more quickly. Each type has its own value chain and economic model.

Closed Loop Cards

Most closed loop cards are gift cards. The sponsor of the card is a merchant, which is trying to drive increased sales.

The figure below shows the basic roles in the closed loop value chain. Roles other than sponsor and bank are optional: a merchant can handle program management and processing in house, and may choose not to use a distributor to have cards sold in other locations.

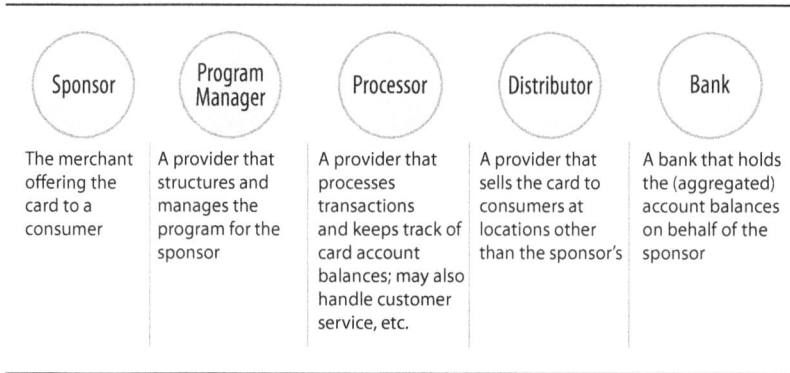

Sponsor	Program Manager	Processor	Distributor	Bank
The merchant offering the card to a consumer	A provider that structures and manages the program for the sponsor	A provider that processes transactions and keeps track of card account balances; may also handle customer service, etc.	A provider that sells the card to consumers at locations other than the sponsor's	A bank that holds the (aggregated) account balances on behalf of the sponsor

Figure 5-7: Prepaid Value Chain—Closed Loop

Gift card programs are often tied into merchant loyalty programs, specialized program managers and processors have designed increasingly intricate product offerings to meet the needs of their sponsor customers. Often, one company provides both program management and processing capabilities.

Gift cards are almost always sold to the consumer at face value. The merchant is looking for increased sales, and considers the expenses paid to others in the value chain a reasonable investment. Some merchants, for example, know that they will benefit each time a gift card recipient makes a purchase larger than the gift card amount.

In the early days, some gift card sponsors attempted to charge "inactivity fees" (decreasing the card balance each month), or assigned expiration dates to the card balance. These practices are becoming much less common, however, as they have provoked consumer outrage and regulatory attention.

The role of the prepaid card distributor is an unusual one in payments systems, but one which has proven to be highly successful for both the distributor and the distributor's outlets (which sell the cards). Prepaid card distributors emerged as supermarkets and convenience stores figured out that they could profit from selling merchant-branded gift cards at their locations. Over time, consumers increasingly expected to be able to choose from a wide range of gift cards at so-called "gift card malls" in supermarkets, and distributors working with retailers enabled them to do so.

Open-loop Cards

Open-loop, or network-branded, prepaid cards are usable wherever that card network brand is accepted—including for purchases, bill payments, and withdrawals of cash at an ATM.

There are dozens of different variations and purposes for open-loop cards. Much of today's innovation in the payment card industry is taking place with open-loop cards.

Segments of this market include:

- Business-to-consumer: rebates, refunds, promotions, insurance claims
- Government-to-consumer: benefits, social security, veterans' compensation
- Employer-to-employee: payroll cards, incentive cards, bonus cards
- Consumer-to-merchant: open-loop gift cards, travel cards, youth cards
- Checking account replacement: as an alternative to a traditional bank checking account (sometimes called GPR or "general purpose reloadable" cards)

As shown below, the value chain and roles are similar to those of closed loop cards, with the important distinction of the network connection.

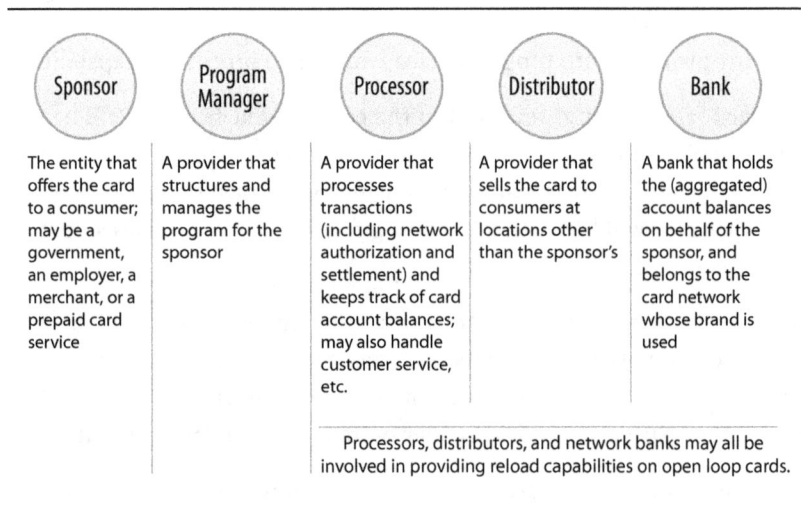

Sponsor	Program Manager	Processor	Distributor	Bank
The entity that offers the card to a consumer; may be a government, an employer, a merchant, or a prepaid card service	A provider that structures and manages the program for the sponsor	A provider that processes transactions (including network authorization and settlement) and keeps track of card account balances; may also handle customer service, etc.	A provider that sells the card to consumers at locations other than the sponsor's	A bank that holds the (aggregated) account balances on behalf of the sponsor, and belongs to the card network whose brand is used

Processors, distributors, and network banks may all be involved in providing reload capabilities on open loop cards.

Figure 5-8: Prepaid Value Chain—Open Loop

Unlike closed loop prepaid cards, the primary motivation is not captive merchant sales at the sponsor's stores. Instead, open-loop prepaid cards are designed to make money for the sponsor—the open-loop card is sold to the consumer with an activation fee on top of the face value of the card, and a long list of additional fees (monthly maintenance, transaction charges, reload charges, etc.) are common. The prepaid card issuer also receives network interchange on purchase transactions.

Prepaid Card Regulation

Because of the newness and growth of prepaid cards, the regulatory environment has been both uncertain and evolving rapidly.

Closed loop cards have been subject to a variety of state laws and, with passage of the Credit Card Act of 2009, new federal regulations. The Act sets new minimum thresholds for fees and expiration dates, but doesn't prevent state laws from being even more restrictive.

> ### A Bank on a Card?
>
> Open-loop prepaid cards have been called "a bank on a card," and prepaid card providers have enhanced the capabilities of cards beyond simple purchases and ATM withdrawals. Often, these cards can accept direct deposit of payroll; can be used for online bill payment; and, increasingly, can be tied to savings accounts and/or limited lines of credit. Some highly specialized open-loop cards, such as healthcare cards, are good at any network merchant, but only for specific categories of spending approved by the sponsor.

Open-loop cards are also subject to regulation, including KYC (know your customer) requirements on the card issuer. Open-loop cards are also subject to Federal Reserve Board Regulation E. Regulators continue to keep a close eye on these cards to prevent their use in money laundering schemes.

The Consumer Financial Protection Bureau also plays an important regulatory role with respect to prepaid cards and is considering new rules that would require new disclosures, error resolution procedures, consumer liability limits for unauthorized transactions, fee limits, and added requirements for cards with overdraft or credit features.

Card Acquiring

> ### Who is an Acquirer?
>
> This term is frequently confusing, in part because there are at least two ways to understand it.
>
> From a **merchant perspective,** the "acquirer" is the entity that sold the merchant a merchant account, and with whom the merchant deals on a day-to-day basis. This may be a bank, a processor, a gateway, or, perhaps most typically, an ISO (independent sales organization).
>
> From a **card network's perspective**, the "acquirer" is the bank that belongs to the card network and has the contractual liability to the network for the actions of its clients in handling payments within that network.
>
> From an **industry perspective,** the "acquirer" is the bank or non-bank processor bundling most of the functions in the value chain, delivered to the merchant either directly or via distribution channels.

The card acquiring side of the industry facilitates acceptance of cards by merchants. It can be a bit difficult to quickly understand because of the variations in roles played by acquiring-side stakeholders. Both processing and economic models vary widely, with significant differences occurring by industry vertical and size of merchant. In this section, we describe core functions and major models in the current market.

The figure below shows the overall acquiring value chain. Core functions within the chain are usually grouped into "Front-End Functions" and "Back-End Functions".

The Card Acquiring Value Chain includes two sets of processes; any provider may perform some or all of these processes.

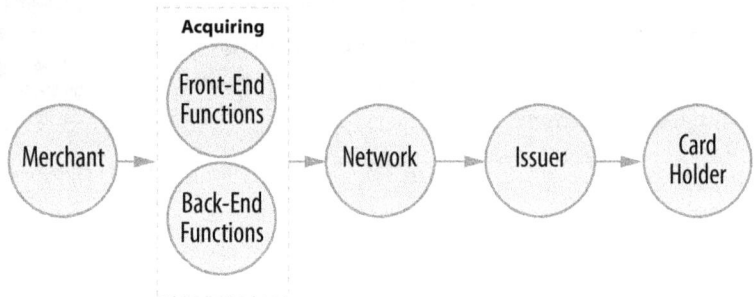

Figure 5-9: The Card Acquiring Value Chain

Roles and Functions in Acquiring

Many types of companies, in different combinations, may perform the roles described in this section. The only hard and fast rule is that the acquiring bank must be a network member. Otherwise, it is common to see both big and small providers offering a variety of services—either bundling services for a merchant, or providing one or more services as a part of a bundle that another company has assembled.

Large merchants are more likely to buy acquiring services on an a-la-carte basis, assembling the bundles themselves. Smaller merchants are much more likely to buy bundles of fully packaged services. The figure below depicts elements of the acquiring value chain.

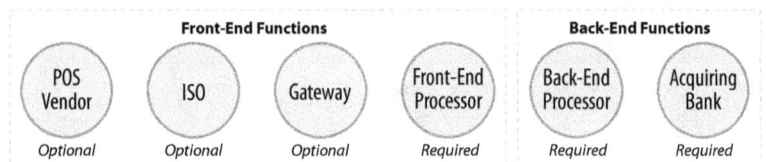

Figure 5-10: Card Acquiring—Specific Functions

- **POS vendor.** Merchants operating at the physical point of sale need a device to accept the card. This can be either a freestanding POS terminal or a software component in an integrated system such as an electronic cash register. Merchants may buy (new or used) POS terminals or use PCs with card swipe capabilities added. Smartphones may also be used as terminals. Acquirers or their ISOs may supply the necessary hardware and software to merchants. Many industry verticals have specialized systems with integrated payments capabilities; for example, a hotel, restaurant, or doctor's office is likely to use a business management system with integrated payments acceptance capability. In some of these verticals, VARs (value-added resellers) play a critical role as authorized distributors of acceptance devices; VARs may also support POS installation and customized software. In the eCommerce domain, the shopping cart provider is the POS vendor.

- **ISO.** A merchant may buy card acceptance from an ISO, or independent sales organization; an ISO can be a one-person operation or a large organization. The ISO may be "captive"—selling merchant services on behalf of a single acquirer—or may shop for processors and acquiring banks and assemble packages of services for merchants. The ISO business model may be a simple sales commission, or may involve a small share of the discount rate revenue earned from the merchant; in some cases, the ISO takes responsibility for any associated merchant credit risk.

> ### Pounding the Pavement
> ISOs have frequently been referred to as "feet on the street" for acquirers. They have played an essential role in reaching small merchants, in particular, for acceptance of card payments.

- **Gateway.** A specialized processor that serves the unique needs of a specific merchant vertical group. Gateways may combine the ISO function as well as other value-added services specific to that industry. In the U.S. market, the eCommerce industry vertical is one major user of gateway services. eCommerce gateways played an important role, early in the development of online retailing, by helping online merchants connect to the proprietary formats and systems of acquiring processors. Because of the unique fraud risks borne by merchants for eCommerce payments, these gateways also developed substantial risk management capabilities. Hotels, restaurants, and airlines are among the other industry verticals that use a variety of gateway services. Gateway fees are typically fixed "cents per transaction" charges.

- **Front-end processor.** Handles authorization message processing for the merchant. This is a real-time processing business, and again tends to be somewhat specialized by industry vertical. The business model here is also a fixed fee. The technical interface to most front-end processors uses proprietary formats, making it difficult for merchants to switch processors. Some gateways provide "insulation" by supporting many different front-end processors, thereby allowing a merchant to switch processors more easily without significant system changes.

- **Back-end processor.** Handles the settlement and clearing messages delivered in batch, most typically at the end of a processing cycle, by the merchant. The back-end processor applies interchange to transactions (including "downgrading" transactions that don't meet the requirements for lower interchange rates) and provides a consolidated financial settlement to the merchant. Chargebacks and disputes come back to the merchant via the back-end processor, and can affect the financial settlement. Reporting to the merchant (helping the merchant reconcile actual with expected receipts) is an important part of the back-end processor's function. In addition, the back-end processor most typically generates the bill for acquiring services that it (or the acquirer that has selected it) sends to the merchant. The business model is a fixed fee per transaction with an additional charge for exception items.

- **Acquiring bank.** Every card network transaction must use an acquiring bank. This bank can be the visible "acquirer" in the market or, at the other extreme, a "rent-a-BIN" bank providing card network access to another entity that is the visible "acquirer" in the market. Even in the latter case, the bank is contractually responsible to the network for the merchant's and processor's actions and conformance to network rules. The acquiring bank's revenue model may be a share of the discount fee or a flat fee for use of the BIN.

Acquiring Competition and Market Share

Competition naturally exists within each of the functions listed above. The large players in the acquiring side of the industry often provide all such functions; other businesses may provide only some, outsourcing other elements of the value chain to different processors (sometimes even to competitors).

The Economics of Acquiring

Given the complexities of the multiple providers and bundles involved, we will now take a step back and describe the overall economics of acquiring. The comments in this section apply to the fees paid by a merchant (to one or more providers) and the costs of servicing a merchant (although the service may be performed by one or more providers).

Acquiring revenue is largely based upon the merchant discount fee—the price charged by the acquirer to the merchant. This is normally expressed as a fixed fee plus a percentage of the value of the transaction. Since card interchange fees (charged by the issuer to the acquirer) are such an important component of acquiring expense, the acquirer often prices services to the merchant on an "interchange plus" basis. A merchant discount fee, therefore, may have a price of "interchange plus assessments" (the card network fee assessed to the acquirer) plus "x cents per transaction plus y% of the transaction value."

Other sources of revenue include float (funds received from the card issuer but not yet paid out to the merchant), monthly fees, and exception handling fees.

The expense side of acquiring includes:

- Interchange fees

- Card network assessments

- Merchant acquisition costs

- Systems development, maintenance, and compliance

- Processing costs

- Merchant servicing costs

- Credit losses

- Fraud losses

> ### Reading the Fine Print
>
> Acquirers' statements to merchants are notoriously complicated and long—a real case of "the devil is in the details." More recently, new entrants such as Square have dramatically simplified merchant statements—and associated pricing and terms.

It may seem surprising that the acquiring side of the business is exposed to credit and fraud losses. But the acquirer is responsible to the card network (which is responsible, in turn, to the issuer) for the good behavior of its merchants. A fraudulent merchant who, as an example ships "empty boxes" or knowingly sells fraudulent goods, will result in cardholder disputes and chargebacks on those transactions back to the merchant. If the merchant has disappeared, or if its account cannot fund the chargebacks, the acquirer bears the financial responsibility. Because of this, fraud management of merchant accounts is an important part of the acquirer's job.

Credit exposure can be an even more serious risk to acquirers. Certain types of merchants, such as airlines and others, sell tickets and receive payment in advance of service delivery. If an airline goes out of business between the time it collected payment from the cardholder and the scheduled use of the ticket, the cardholder will often, under the card network rules, be able to charge back the transaction for services not received. The financial obligation in this case falls on the acquirer. Because of this risk, many acquirers demand hefty guarantees, or hold funds in escrow, for at-risk merchants and merchant categories—or simply choose not to service those merchants/categories because of the potential credit risk.

Card Risk Management

Risk in card systems takes many forms and touches all stakeholders in one form or another. The two primary forms of risk are credit risk and fraud risk. On an industry-wide basis, fraud losses are much smaller than credit losses.

Credit Risk

A credit card issuer is obviously taking on credit risk when extending a line of credit to a new cardholder. Issuers control this risk through a credit approval process at the time of account opening, and via periodic reviews of the cardholder's account and behavior.

Credit bureaus are a critical component of the credit risk management process: they provide a comprehensive view of a cardholder's credit exposures and payment behavior with multiple lenders. Credit bureaus and card issuers have become increasingly sophisticated in using—and automating—the tasks of reviewing a cardholder's status and deciding on actions (increasing or decreasing lines, sending an account to collection, etc.). Credit bureaus, issuers, and third parties use scoring techniques to evaluate a cardholder's potential for loan repayment. In recent years, credit bureaus have developed products that can deliver credit scores on potential new cardholders in real-time, thereby enabling "instant issuance" of credit card accounts.

Charge card issuers also take credit risk, but for a shorter time period, as cardholders are expected to repay account balances at the end of each billing period.

Debit card issuers take no credit risk unless they authorize a transaction against insufficient funds, thereby approving an overdraft loan to the consumer. In doing so, they have credit risk exposure similar to that of the charge card issuer—though the consumer is expected to repay the overdraft quickly, usually within the next day.

Prepaid card issuers take no credit risk, as card system rules do not permit the extension of overdraft protection to prepaid cardholders.

Fraud Risk

Credit and debit card fraud, and fraud risk management, is a highly developed science—on the part of fraudsters and the card issuers, acquirers, and merchants that manage the fraud risk. There are a few important concepts to recognize in understanding card fraud:

Fighting card fraud requires sophisticated analysis techniques—and real data. One of the most important functions played by the card networks in this area is the accumulation of fraud data from issuers (issuers must report fraud when discovered), and the analysis of that data.

Card fraud is responsive to efforts to control it, although it mutates. When the industry identifies a fraud technique as significant enough to merit a concentrated response against that form of fraud, actions are taken to drive it down. Almost always, however, fraud pops up again with another technique, or a different angle or target.

Credit card issuers have learned that it works best to band together and share resources in fighting fraud. The card networks play a primary role in facilitating those efforts. (Credit risk, on the other hand, is dealt with very much on an issuer-by-issuer basis, and managing credit risk is seen as a key competitive differentiator.)

For both credit and debit cards, there is a major difference in rules between card-present and card-not-present environments. At a macro level, card network rules allocate fraud liability to the card issuer in card-present acceptance environments, while the fraud liability in card-not-present acceptance environments is allocated to the card acquirer (and, therefore, is ultimately borne by the card-not-present merchant). If a cardholder claims, "I didn't do it," (that is, I didn't make the purchase that appears on the statement) and the transaction occurred at a physical store, then, when the cardholder's account is credited, the card issuer bears the loss—the merchant keeps the sale. In a similar situation, if the transaction occurs at an online retailer, the card issuer can charge back the transaction to the acquirer—which then debits the merchant's account.

There are exceptions to these macro level rules for fraud assignment. Transaction fraud in the card-not-present acceptance environment, for example, shifts fraud liability from the merchant to the issuer when the merchant uses the 3D Secure "buyer authentication" protocol. Transaction fraud

> ### Who Needs Signature?
>
> Card networks have recently eliminated the signature requirement for many merchant category codes for purchases—no signature is required for purchases under $15 when conducted in an unattended environment, under $25 when conducted in a face-to-face environment, and under $50 when conducted in discount stores or supermarkets. Convenience and speed of payment trumps any potential increase in fraud.

in the card-present acceptance environments, likewise, shifts fraud liability from the issuer to the merchant if the merchant is required to capture the cardholder's signature but fails to do so.

Types of Card Fraud and Fraud Control Mechanisms

- **Lost and stolen fraud.** Someone other than an authorized individual uses a legitimate card account in a card-present environment. The earliest and most basic defense introduced to deal with this type of fraud was signature checking. Recognizing the limitations of this as a control, issuers (or their processors) use sophisticated decisioning tools as part of their authorization systems, to try to detect unusual and suspect transactions. When a cardholder reports a lost or stolen card, the account is closed, subsequent authorizations are denied, and a replacement card is sent to the cardholder. The ultimate step to mitigate lost and stolen fraud is to mandate the use of PINs for cards—something that is not currently required in the U.S. market.

- **Counterfeit fraud.** The card's magnetic stripe data has been duplicated on a new piece of plastic and is used by a fraudster. This very popular fraud was particularly easy to pull off in the early days of credit cards, when a counterfeit card could be created from just the data visible on the card (name, expiration date, account number). In the 1980s, to counter increasing counterfeit fraud, the card networks enhanced the mag stripe with the addition of the CVN, a security code in the magnetic track that does not appear physically on the card itself. As a result, to create a counterfeit, a fraudster must read the mag stripe ("skimming") or intercept a stored image of it. In recent years, the PCI-DSS standards have imposed a stringent requirement on industry stakeholders preventing storage of any mag stripe data—because of the significant value of stripe data to counterfeiters. Another defense against counterfeit fraud is the authorization decisioning systems mentioned above. In today's market, the card system is moving to chip cards, which should make counterfeit fraud much more difficult for fraudsters.

> **The Stripe Stays**
>
> Dealing with counterfeit fraud is one of the primary arguments for adopting chip card technology in lieu of magnetic stripes. However, as long as the card also has a magnetic stripe, and can be used in acceptance markets with just that stripe, it is not a perfect defense. Indeed, counterfeit fraud can be expected to migrate to those magnetic stripe-only acceptance locations.

- **Card not received fraud.** A newly issued card stolen en route to the legitimate cardholder and used by a fraudster. This form of fraud has been successfully countered by requiring cardholders to call the card issuer to authenticate themselves and activate a new account.

- **Identity theft.** A card account has been fraudulently opened in the name of another consumer (real or fictitious). Card issuers rely on a number of shared databases, operated by the card networks and by third parties, to identify potentially fraudulent new account applications. Such a database might highlight, for example, a phone number associated with a previously identified fraudulent account.

- **Identity creation.** A fictitious identity has been created, and a card account opened in the name of the fictitious person. Again, the control against this is the use of shared negative identity databases.

- **Unauthorized use.** In this form of fraud, a legitimate card account is used by an unauthorized individual in a card-not-present environment (Internet, mail, or telephone order). The risk in this case is borne by the card-accepting merchant, not the card issuer. Merchants use a wide variety of techniques—both internal and third-party services—to identify potentially fraudulent transactions. One popular method is the use of address verification services provided by the card networks. The three-digit CVN security code that appears on the signature panel of a card is sometimes requested by the merchant to provide some proof of physical possession of the card.

- **"Bust out" fraud.** A legitimate card account is used by an individual who has no intent to pay off the balance. This type of fraud is controlled with the same tools used to monitor credit risk exposures.

- **PIN debit fraud.** The rules of the PIN debit networks require hardware-encrypted devices for PIN entry, to verify the consumer. As a result, fraud in card-present environments is limited. When it does occur, it is typically because of theft of both the PIN and the physical card. In one scenario, a fake ATM front accepts and reads the magnetic stripe of a debit card, while a hidden camera records the PIN entry.

Data Security and PCI

The growing sophistication of fraudsters in hacking computer networks and stealing payment card data has created a huge problem for the card payment industry. Processing system intrusions have compromised millions of card accounts simultaneously. In addition to leading to fraudulent card usage, these attacks have been costly for issuers (which must both handle the public relations issues and decide whether to reissue cards on potentially compromised accounts) and detrimental to the industry as a whole (as they reduce consumer confidence in the integrity of the card systems).

> ### Big Dollars
>
> Some industry experts have estimated total cost of PCI-DSS compliance in the United States, on the part of all parties in the industry, at several billion dollars. Merchants and processors are also realizing that these compliance costs are not one-time events, and that "security is a journey, not a destination." Some merchants are moving toward—or thinking about—PaaS, or payments as a service, as a way of outsourcing the entire payments process, thereby reducing PCI "scope" and the associated costs of PCI-DSS compliance.

But the primary weight of addressing the problem has fallen on the shoulders of merchants and their acquirers. Most such attacks have been made on merchant payments acceptance systems, or on acquirers or processors. To combat this problem, the card networks joined forces to form PCI-DSS—the Payment Card Industry Data Security Standard. Known as PCI, it is a set of requirements designed to protect cardholder data on merchant and processor systems.

Following agreement on the requirements to drive compliance, the card networks began to require compliance assessment for stakeholders, and to fine violating merchants and processors—sometimes significantly. PCI compliance is an important step, but it is becoming evident that attacks are still possible. Several other initiatives are underway to further protect card data, including tokenization (see below) and end-to-end encryption (to protect card data from being entered into point of sale acceptance locations).

As data breaches continued to proliferate even in the face of increasing PCI-DSS compliance, the card networks also implemented additional fines and assessments used to help card issuers cover some of their costs associated with card re-issuance following exposure of cards in a data breach. In one major data breach, the CEO of the merchant involved ultimately resigned as the company's sales were affected by a loss of consumer confidence in shopping at that merchant. Protection of card credentials is serious business—with serious consequences when failures occur.

To help address the data breach issue, the card industry has also embarked on joint initiatives to reduce or eliminate the storage of card credentials. These initiatives—called "tokenization"—involve the use of alias or proxy card numbers which have limited utility and, even if compromised, will result in significantly lower levels of potential fraud loss. Apple Pay was one of the first adopters of this tokenization technology and uses it to store a totally different card number in the mobile device than is on the cardholder's card. The card networks play a critical role by both defining the standards for tokenization to work as well as providing the translation layer between a tokenized number and the real number known to the card issuer.

Summary: Cards

The card payments systems in the United States have shown dramatic growth for both consumer and business payments, and offer significant utility to both users (cardholders, merchants) and providers (networks, processors, banks) of the systems.

In many ways because of their success, card systems are likely to see, however, increasing regulatory oversight, ongoing pressure on interchange, and competition from alternative products and providers.

Key Trends in Cards

- Continued concentration among credit card issuers

- Continued growth of debit transaction volume at the expense of cash and checks

- New regulatory pressures on both credit and debit issuers—providing increased consumer protection

- New financial pressures on "regulated" debit issuers as a result of Federal Reserve imposition of reduced interchange fees and network routing requirements

- Ongoing debate, litigation, and regulation about merits and levels of card interchange

- New form factors: chip, contactless, mobile, etc.

- New mobile POS acceptance environments using smartphones, tablets, etc. and a migration away from purpose-built POS devices

- Continued support of rewards programs for credit

Sources of Information—Cards

- PaymentsNews.com

- The Nilson Report

- Visa, Mastercard, American Express, Discover Financial Services

- Philadelphia Federal Reserve Bank Payments Card Center

Core Systems: Cash

Type	"Push" payments
Ownership	No ownership
Regulation	U.S. law and Federal Reserve Bank regulation
Network Economics	ATM withdrawals subject to network interchange

Table 6-1: Cash Overview

Cash is, in many ways, the simplest of the payments systems in the United States. As a self-clearing "push" payments system, it has none of the complexities of either open or closed loop systems. It is a non-account based system: neither the payee nor the payer need to have any kind of account or service relationship with a provider in order to use it. It is a virtual payments system—no one owns it, and no one writes "the rules" for cash. Interestingly, it is the only form of payment that can be used anonymously on the part of both payer and payee. Perhaps because of this simplicity, it remains both the most commonly used form of payment and, often, the least understood. In this chapter we will explore how cash gets into the economy, what's involved in its use and circulation, and who profits from the system.

Cash Volumes

No one really knows the true number of cash transactions in the U.S. economy. Estimates have been made (most recently, by the San Francisco Federal Reserve Bank) for the volume of U.S. consumer payments made by cash. But there obviously is no way to systematically count person-to-person transactions. The same is true for many payments to small or personal businesses, as well as cash payrolls paid to temporary or "off-the-books" employees. There is, of course, significant cash usage within the criminal economy. Finally, some economists estimate that as much as 60% of cash produced by the U.S. is actually held overseas.

> **Lots of Cash**
>
> In *Greenback*, his book about cash, Jason Goodwin notes, "There are more dollar bills in existence than any other branded object, including Coke cans."

Cash Production and Supply

Cash is physically produced by the U.S. Treasury's Bureau of Engraving and Printing (bank notes) and the U.S. Mint (coins). The only way that cash can get physically inserted into the economy is if a bank that is a Federal Reserve Bank member orders cash from the Fed. Upon receiving the order, the Fed debits the bank's account at the Fed for the amount ordered, and tells the bank to come and collect the cash.

Banks then need to deliver the cash to their vaults at branches, to their ATMs, and to merchants that have put in orders for cash; armored car services supply the trucks and the personnel to do this on behalf of the banks.

Cash gets into the economy when a Federal Reserve Bank member bank buys cash from the Fed. End Party then receives cash from banks through branches or ATMs.

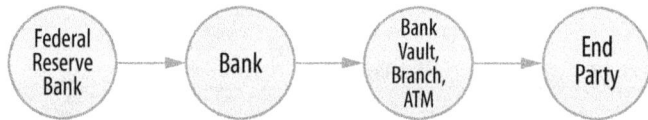

Figure 6-1: The Cash Value Chain

Cash Acceptance

Merchants that accept cash need to have the personnel and secure storage systems to handle it, as well as procedures and systems to control both employee and customer theft.

The cost of cash acceptance by merchants varies according to the type of merchant and the size of the cash payments. There are very few variable costs associated with cash: cash handling, depositing, and fraud (theft) control expenses are largely fixed. One result of this is that a merchant who reduces the percentage of cash payments is unlikely to see a corresponding reduction in expense.

Cash Deposit

Consumers and enterprises deposit cash at banks. Banks need to be able to count and securely store the cash. Some banks accept cash deposits at ATMs as well as at branches. Many banks offer late-night deposit vaults for businesses needing to deposit end-of-day proceeds. Banks charge enterprises for frequent or large cash deposit activities. A large cash-accepting merchant will often count, wrap, and bundle cash prior to deposit in order to reduce these fees. Recently, banks have been offering larger merchants "onsite vaults": the merchant deposits cash into a secure vault, which (somewhat like an ATM) counts and verifies the cash; the cash is then deemed to have been deposited into the bank, which periodically has the cash picked up by an armored car service.

Grocery stores and other high-frequency, cash-accepting merchants "recycle" cash by providing cash back at the point of sale to customers paying with their PIN debit card.

Banks also routinely screen currency to detect counterfeits (as do some large merchants); most counterfeit currency is caught in this manner.

Banks themselves can deposit excess, worn, or damaged currency at the Federal Reserve Bank; worn or damaged currency is then destroyed.

Cash in the Emerging Markets

In many developing countries, cash is the dominant form of payment. In India, for example, one researcher estimated that 96% of all purchases are made by cash. This is, of course, in large part because of the high percentage (often over 90%) of residents who are "unbanked." In many of these countries, relatively formal cash-transfer networks have evolved—these are sometimes known as hawala networks.

Because of the dominance of cash, emerging mobile wallet services (such as the well-known M-Pesa service in Kenya) rely heavily on agents—small shopkeepers who are registered as agents of the mobile wallet service—to provide CICO: "cash-in" and "cash-out" services. So a city worker, for example, might want to use a mobile wallet to transfer money to his mother in a rural village. He would go to an agent, deposit cash ("cash-in"), and receive electronic credit in his wallet. He would then transfer the electronic credit to his mother's wallet. She, in turn, would go to a local agent, deposit the electronic credit, and receive spendable cash in return ("cash-out").

In many developing markets, as well as in more developed, but cash-centric markets, "cash to online voucher" services have been developed, to help cash-centric consumers make purchases online.

ATMs and ATM Networks

ATMs are the most common way that U.S. consumers get cash from their bank accounts. ATMs were introduced in the U.S. first in the 1970s, primarily to reduce branch operations expenses, but also to provide convenience to customers.

Today, ATMs are operated by banks, both on their own premises and "off-premises," and by non-banks. With current ATM network interoperability, a consumer in the U.S. can generally get cash from almost any ATM—although fees may be involved if the consumer isn't using one of their bank's ATMs. The figure below depicts the ATM value chain.

A consumer may withdraw cash (1) from his or her own bank; (2) from another bank, which connects to the consumer's bank through an ATM network; or (3) from a non-bank, which connects to the consumer's bank through a relationship with another bank (which, in turn, belongs to an ATM network).

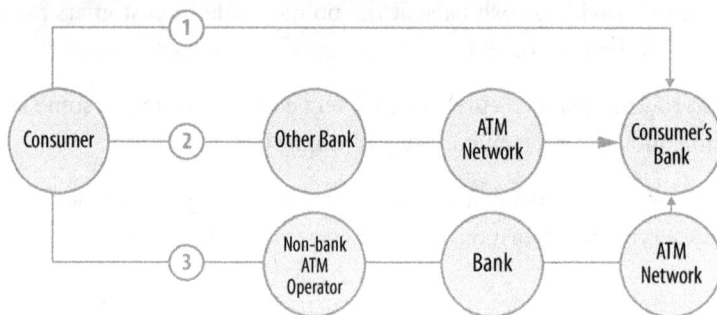

Figure 6-2: The ATM Value Chain

There is a fairly complex flow of fees found in the ATM industry.

- A bank may charge a customer for withdrawing cash from its own ATMs, but this is atypical; most often, ATM withdrawals (perhaps up to a monthly limit) are included in the bank's checking account "package"

- If a customer goes to another bank's ATM to withdraw cash, a number of fees may apply:

  — The ATM network that connects the two banks sets an interchange fee, which the customer's bank pays to the bank whose ATM was used. (This can be thought of as "backward interchange", as it flows away from the customer's bank, rather than toward it as for POS debit transactions.)

  — The bank whose ATM is used may assess a fee (the "surcharge"), which is taken out of the customer's account, along with the withdrawal.

  — The customer's bank may assess a fee to its own customer for using a foreign ATM; this is intended to offset the interchange that the bank had to pay on that transaction.

- If a customer goes to a non-bank ATM, the fees are similar to those above. The non-bank ATM must contract with an ATM network member bank in order to connect to the customer's bank account. The non-bank ATM owner and the bank it contracts with reach an agreement to share the revenue from the customer (the surcharge) and the revenue from the customer's bank (the interchange).

- One or more of the bank or non-bank ATM owners may contract with a processor to provide network access, or to service its ATMs ("ATM driving"). A facility owner (a store, for example) may also be paid for hosting the ATM.

There are a number of "surcharge-free" ATM networks in the U.S. A bank (or prepaid card issuer) joining one of these networks enables its customer to withdraw cash at a network ATM without being exposed to surcharges by the other bank. The other bank still receives interchange from the customer's bank.

Cash Regulation and Risk Management

Because of extensive use of cash in the criminal economy, there is a significant amount of regulation around cash deposits. The Bank Secrecy Act of 1970, and later the USA PATRIOT Act of 2001, created obligations on the part of banks to report large cash deposits, in order to reduce money laundering. Banks that fail to comply face significant fines.

Counterfeit currency is an ever-evolving fraud problem. Technological advances in imaging and printing have made counterfeiting easier; as a result, banks and processors have installed ever more sophisticated counterfeit detection equipment. The U.S. Secret Service has law enforcement responsibility for prevention and investigation of counterfeiting of U.S. currency.

Major Providers

Major industry providers are listed in the table below.

Banks	ATM Manufacturers
The Federal Reserve	Diebold
Cash Delivery Services	NCR
Loomis	Non-Bank ATMs
Garda	Cardtronics
Brinks	Payment Alliance
Anti-Money Laundering Software	Surcharge-Free Networks
Oracle/Mantis	Allpoint (Cardtronics)
Actimize/Fortent	MoneyPass
Counterfeit Detection Hardware	
AceDepot	
Not all providers or all categories are listed	

Table 6-2: Major Providers—Cash Services

Summary: Cash

The cash payments system's grip on small-value transactions appears to be finally loosening with the widespread acceptance of card payments. The advantages of simplicity, convenience, and anonymity will, however, continue to make it a significant force in the world of payments.

Key Trends in Cash

- Use of cash falling at POS
- On-premise merchant cash vaults as bank deposits
- Envelope-free ATMs leading to increased ATM deposit activity
- Unbanked consumers with open loop prepaid cards driving ATM volumes up

Sources of Information—Cash

- PaymentsNews.com
- The Federal Reserve Bank Payments Services
- The Federal Reserve Bank of San Francisco
- Bureau of Engraving and Printing—U.S. Department of the Treasury
- U.S. Mint
- NAAIO (ATM association)
- EFTA

Core Systems: Wire Transfer

Type	"Push" payments
Ownership	Fedwire: Federal Reserve Bank CHIPS: The Clearing House
Regulation	Federal Reserve Bank regulation and private network rules
Network Economics	Clears at par
Processing	Electronic, real-time
Risk Management	Managed by networks, intermediaries, and end parties

Table 7-1: Wire Transfer Overview

Wire transfer systems carry the serious money in the U.S. payments systems. Also known as "large-value systems," the U.S. wire transfer systems, and their counterparts throughout the world, are designed to handle very high-value transactions between businesses, and most often between financial institutions.

Unlike most industrialized countries, the U.S. has two such systems: Fedwire and CHIPS. An important third system, SWIFT, is not a payments system, but a global financial services messaging system, frequently used in conjunction with the large-value systems.

Most large-value systems worldwide have been modified over the past twenty years to become real-time gross settlement (RTGS) systems. These systems do not use the "net settlement" process typical of all paper and electronic consumer systems, instead settling each transaction individually in real-time as it occurs. This gross settlement is necessary to avoid the risks associated with a potential bank failure. With hundreds of billions, and sometimes trillions, of dollars transferred daily, a net settlement system would expose the network—and therefore the network owners—to intolerable risks even if only one member bank failed during the day.

> **The Legacy of Herstatt risk**
>
> The failure of the German bank, Herstatt, in 1974, during the course of a day, caused huge losses worldwide and a cascade of bank failures. This type of risk, which became known as "Herstatt risk," led to the development of RTGS and CLS (continuous linked settlement) systems worldwide.

Volumes

Large-value systems account for a small fraction of payments systems transactions but a very large percentage of the dollar value. In large part, this is because of the financial transactions (such as foreign exchange transactions and securities settlements) that flow through the networks.

Uses and Purposes

Wire transfers are commonly used for:

- Time-critical payments such as large-value purchases with specific payment dates.

- Fully guaranteed payments. A wire transfer cannot be repudiated, reversed, or charged back without the agreement of the recipient.

- Immediate payments, for example, for the sale of a security or the settlement of a trade.

Financial institutions, including banks and securities firms, routinely use wire transfers for the settlement of financial market transactions. Businesses make some, but not most, of their supplier payments via wire transfer. Consumers rarely use wire transfers, with the exception of transactions such as real estate purchases.

The Value Chain

The sender of funds instructs his or her bank to send a wire transfer to a receiver. The value chain below shows both banks belonging to the same wire transfer network. In other cases, the sender's bank or the receiver's bank (or both) execute the transaction through correspondent relationships with banks that belong to the network.

Sender of Funds → Sender's Bank → Wire Transfer Network → Receiver's Bank → Receiver of Funds

Figure 7-1: The Wire Transfer Value Chain

Fedwire

Fedwire is a service of the Federal Reserve Banks. It is available to banks that have an account at one of the Federal Reserve Banks. (All nationally-chartered banks must have an account at a Federal Reserve Bank, and state-chartered banks have the option of opening such an account.) Fedwire is, in essence, a "super-sized" online banking service.

The wire transfer value chain (shown in the figure above) is deceptively simple. As an example, an enterprise wanting to send a wire transfer sends an electronic message to its bank. Once the bank is satisfied that their customer's request is legitimate, the bank debits the account and sends a message to Fedwire. The Federal Reserve Bank at which the account is domiciled debits the bank's account and credits the account of the receiving bank. The receiving bank then credits the account of the receiving company. All of this is done online, in real time. Of course, the electronic messaging is done with a high degree of security, usually (depending on the type of connection, and bank risk management policies) including encryption and the use of token-based authentication devices. Many companies also opt to have wire transfers above certain limits be subject to dual internal approvals.

The core management problem for all value chain participants is risk. Before sending the instruction to the Fed, the sending bank must be certain that there are good funds in its customer's account. Before crediting the receiving bank, the Fed must be absolutely sure that there are good funds in the sending bank's account. Thousands of transactions and hundreds of millions of dollars flow through these systems on a daily basis, and it is critically important to avoid mistakes.

If the sending company does not have sufficient funds in its account, but is expecting incoming funds shortly to cover the transaction, its bank may extend a daylight overdraft. This is a loan; if the incoming funds never materialize, the bank must collect funds from their customer or face a loss. Similarly, the Fed may extend a daylight overdraft loan to the sending bank. Together, the participants in the system watch the flow of funds and, in particular, try to manage blockages; a failure of one bank to promptly credit its customer's accounts with incoming transfers will result in an inability to process outbound transfers.

CHIPS

CHIPS, or the Clearing House Interbank Payments System, is a private sector alternative to Fedwire. CHIPS is owned by The Clearing House, which in turn is owned by large banks in the United States. It is similar to Fedwire in being a real-time, fully guaranteed system meant to handle high-value payments. Unlike Fedwire, however, which is accessible to any bank with an account at a Federal Reserve Bank, CHIPS is used by only a small number of very large banks. CHIPS is not an RTGS system, using instead a form of multilateral netting that manages settlement risk while providing certain liquidity benefits to participating members.

SWIFT

SWIFT can be thought of as "the payments system that isn't a payments system." SWIFT is a global messaging network for the financial services industry, through which participating members, including banks and securities firms, can send each other secure, structured messages. Many of these messages are payments-related; one might instruct a financial institution to initiate a payments transaction in a wire transfer or other type of payment network. SWIFT has recently opened up its messaging network, allowing corporations to use it to deliver instructions or receive data from participating banks, without the need to maintain separate connections to each bank.

Wire Transfer Regulation and Risk Management

Wire transfer transactions are governed by Article 4A of the Uniform Commercial Code, and by the operating rules of the network (Fedwire or CHIPS).

Risk management, particularly the prevention of fraud, is very important for wire transfer services. Consumer payments systems, both paper and electronic, tolerate a certain amount of fraud. The cost of these fraud losses is covered by the revenue (fees, interchange, interest, float) earned on good transactions. But this doesn't work with wire transfer systems: there is no price a bank can set on a "good" wire transfer that would cover the bank for the loss, for example, on a single fraudulent $500 million transaction. So participants in the value chain, particularly the banks and network operators, surround the network with a complex (and expensive) web of risk management systems, procedures, and people.

Economics

Wire transfer economics are very different from those of consumer payments systems. The incremental cost of processing transactions is relatively low—the Fed, for example, normally charges a fee of well below a dollar to process a transaction through Fedwire. (The exact cost depends on volume—the Fed publishes its price schedule on its website.) The banks, however, charge their customers—both on the sending and receiving side—fees that can range from $3 to $50, again depending on the bank's relationship with their customer and the volume of transactions processed. The difference between the incremental cost of processing through Fedwire and the price to customers reflects the expense associated with maintaining the risk management systems described above, as well as supporting secure connectivity to the bank.

Wire transfer systems, like all "open loop" payments systems, have "on-us" transactions—where the sending bank and the receiving bank are the same. Since wire transfers are particularly concentrated among the largest banks that provide transaction services to the largest financial institutions (other banks, investment banks, brokers, etc.), a higher-than-normal percentage of transactions may be assumed to be "on-us." So when you look at the transaction numbers reported by the Fed and CHIPS, you need to make an assumption about the additional number that do not flow through the Fed or CHIPS, but are kept in-house by the sending institution as an "on-us."

Major Providers

Major industry providers are listed in the table below.

Banks	Networks
Bank of America	Fedwire
JPMorgan Chase	CHIPS
Citibank	*Software & Services*
Wells Fargo	Fundtech
BNY/Mellon	ACI Worldwide
ABN AMRO	FIS/Sungard
Not all providers or all categories are listed.	

Table 7-2: Major Providers—Wire Transfer

In addition to the network providers, the wire transfer industry has traditionally been dominated by what have been called the "Money Center Banks"—the New York City-based banks that provided banking services to Wall Street firms. That concept is somewhat dated now but the same banks still hold leading market share positions in the wire transfer business. Many run significant correspondent banking businesses, and connecting smaller correspondent banks to the wire transfer systems is an important piece of that business.

Summary: Wire Transfer

The wire transfer systems have an unchallenged position in handling financial market transactions. The future may show increased use of wires for commercial, and possibly consumer, transactions.

Key Trends in Wire Transfer

- Wire transfer networks are enhancing their ability to carry remittance data along with payments, in order to further penetrate the B2B supplier payment market.

- More trade is cross-border, and bank wire transfer services are increasingly helping corporate customers manage delivery of cross-border payments to other countries, as well as managing associated foreign exchange transactions.

Sources of Information — Wire Transfer

- The Clearing House—CHIPS
- Federal Reserve Bank Payments Services—Fedwire
- Association for Finance Professionals (AFP)
- SWIFT (Society for Worldwide Interbank Financial Telecommunication)
- SIFMA (Securities Industry and Financial Markets Association)

Perspectives on Payments: System Users

THIS CHAPTER BEGINS A two-part look at the stakeholders that participate in any payments system. First, we'll explore the user perspective—looking at what's most important to the senders and receivers of the funds that
flow in any payments system. Here we'll examine the traditional consumer
and merchant stakeholders, plus take a look at enterprises including businesses, billers, governments, and nonprofits.

In the next chapter, we'll continue our look at stakeholder perspectives—
from the point of view of the providers of each payments system, including
the banks, networks and clearing houses, processors, and payments services
providers that play such a major role in enabling and operating our payments systems.

The Consumer Perspective

With more than 321 million people now residing in the United States, the
U.S. has the world's third-largest population—yet it represents only about
4.5% of the world's total population. The Census Bureau projects a U.S.
population of 439 million by the year 2050. China (19.7%) and India (17.2%)
are each several times larger, with Indonesia, the fourth largest (3.4%), just
behind the U.S.

The U.S. is organized into more than 115 million households, about 87 million of which have traditional bank accounts. About 10 million households,
or 17 million adults, make up a group often called "the unbanked." Another
20 million households (45 million adults) are "underbanked," according to
the FDIC.

Using FDIC definitions, "unbanked" refers to people who rarely, if ever,
have held a checking, savings, or "other type of transaction or check-cashing

account at an insured depository institution in the conventional finance system." The "underbanked", on the other hand, have held bank or credit union accounts, but also rely on alternative payments and financial services, including check cashing services, payday loans, and the purchase of money orders.

From a payments systems perspective, the banking industry looks at consumers through a "household" lens, with the basic depository account often jointly owned by household heads.

Shifting Consumer Payments Behavior

Across the multiple domains of payments touched by individuals, consumer behavior continues to shift and change. Multiple studies have shown the shift to all forms of electronic payments and, in particular, the dramatic growth in debit card transaction volume—most commonly understood as replacing cash and checks. The table below shows, over a ten-year span, this radical shift in consumer payments behavior:

Consumer Payments Transactions – U.S. Market (2002-2011)

As a percent of total "count"

	2002	2006	2011
Debit Cards	13.3%	23.2%	35.9%
Credit Cards	17.1%	18.4%	16.2%
Checks	24.3%	18.6%	10.3%
Cash	42.5%	34.9%	31.4%

Source: Glenbrook

Table 8-1: Consumer Use of Payments Systems

For example, at the point of sale for traditional purchases from local merchants, consumers increasingly prefer to pay with debit cards—shifting rapidly from cash and checks, in particular. For everyday purchases, consumers also prefer debit cards over credit cards—although certain affluent segments, particularly conscious of credit card rewards, continue to be loyal to those cards. With the rapid adoption of smartphones and the availability of new mobile payment options, consumers are beginning to make payments using their phones—especially at familiar, frequently visited locations.

In remote commerce, historically the sole province of credit and debit cards, consumers are increasingly taking advantage of alternative payment options. In some segments of the population, behavior shifts seem to be driven primarily by consumer concerns about the safety of online shopping; others aren't concerned, feeling adequately protected by their payment card zero-liability guarantees.

For recurring bill payments, consumers are shifting away from writing checks to either bill payment services (typically provided by banks as an adjunct to the checking account) or paying at the biller's website using a debit or credit card or, in some cases, via ACH.

A few consumers are taking advantage of new services that allow person-to-person payments to, for example, settle a lunch tab or send money to children away at college. This is an area of particular focus for several mobile payments providers and, increasingly, for major banks that have teamed together to create bank-owned services for person-to-person payments. A challenge for both banks and other providers is monetizing their person-to-person offerings for domestic payments.

For receiving wages, most consumers instruct their employers to send payroll funds via ACH ("direct deposit") directly into their checking account. For certain segments of underbanked consumers, payroll cards provide another option—allowing them to avoid the fees associated with using retail check cashing services to cash their payroll checks.

Over time, the cumulative effects of these changes in consumer behavior will result in checks being a much smaller component of consumer payments, cash usage similarly declining, and card payments (especially debit cards but also credit cards) increasing in importance. Mobile payments are likely to accelerate as consumers become more comfortable with making payments using their smartphones—while the underlying payments are carried out on the credit and debit card systems.

Factors Affecting Consumer Payments Behavior

Many factors play into the decision made by a consumer each time he or she needs to exchange value with another party—including practical considerations such as cost, convenience, familiarity, and frequency of use; earning rewards; taking advantage of credit extension; and timing of the payment. Other factors also play a role, including privacy/security sensitivities, perception of status, and influences from respected others.

Of all of these factors, rewards-based loyalty programs have had perhaps the greatest impact on the increased use of credit cards over the last ten years. The convenience of debit cards has also led to a significant decline in the use of checks to pay for purchases at the point of sale.

Gen Y	Gen X	Boomers	Seniors
Born 1975–2005	*1965–1974*	*1946–1964*	*Before 1946*
Debit card generation	Prefer debit over credit	Strong credit card orientation	Checks/cash orientation
Most likely to bank online	Strong use of all online services	Peak earning and spending power	Not sure about this ATM thing
Most likely to research and buy products online	Expect total transparency of products and services	Have the most credit cards, home equity loans, etc.	Credit card for emergencies
Living the mobile lifestyle	Adopting mobile	Prefer branch for major transactions	Branch banking for almost all transactions
			Phones are for talking

Table 8-2: Consumer Payments Behavior— Demographics

As illustrated in the table above, demographics—particularly age-related factors—have been shown to influence consumer payment behavior. For example, younger individuals living a mobile lifestyle tend to be heavy users of debit cards, dislike checks, and bank and shop online. Baby boomers, at their peak in terms of earning and spending power, tend to be more rewards-oriented; many pay off their credit card charges every month. Seniors tend to be the last bastion of checks, may still lack confidence in ATMs, and darken the bank branch doorways regularly!

Perhaps more telling than demographics, however, are the psychographic effects associated with consumer decisions about payments as illustrated in the table above. We all have various emotional relationships to money, and our decisions aren't always rational as a result. For example, some individuals, more carefree by nature, are much less worried about security than others who tend to be ultra-careful in their choices. Others are very cost-sensitive—even irrespective of their actual economic status. These psychographic factors result in it being difficult to anticipate consumer choices based on just demographics.

"Carefree"	"Careful"
Only one of many possible sets of profiles!	
Don't keep track of balances	Keep track of account balances, limits and expenditures
Pay bills when due—or later	Pay bills on schedule
May overdraw accounts or exceed limits	Don't overdraw
Pursue rewards only for the goodies	Pursue rewards even if not redeemed
Less security conscious	More security conscious
High convenience orientation	High financial rewards orientation

Table 8-3: Consumer Payments Behavior— Psychographics

Glenbrook's Theory on Consumer Adoption of New Payments Mechanisms

At Glenbrook, we've developed a simple theory about what really matters in shaping consumer behavior around new ways to pay: big increases in convenience and/or big perceived financial gains. Almost nothing else seems to matter.

Convenience helps instill confidence and inspires frequent usage. Anything that gets in the way of convenience—call it "friction"—is likely to dramatically reduce potential consumer acceptance. Said differently, consumers rarely move to alternative ways to pay that are less convenient.

Financial gains can also frequently drive changes in payments systems preferences. But financial gains have to be significant to matter to consumers—significant enough to overcome existing habits and preferences about ways to pay. Rich rewards programs have demonstrated their ability to significantly influence consumer loyalty to a particular payment card, for example.

One topic continues to confound payments providers. Consumers often say they care about security, and want more secure payment solutions—but often fail to adopt them when offered the option! Our conclusion is that security matters—consumers expect payments systems to be secure—but extra security doesn't lead to extra adoption.

At the end of the day, we must not forget that making a payment is not the consumer's real focus. Rather, consumers want to own the products they're purchasing, or experience the service, or pay off a liability incurred to another. That's where the rewards are—not in the payment mechanism itself!

Consumer Payments Markets We're Watching

As keen observers of the payments scene, we're particularly watching consumer adoption of new payments products and services for person-to-person payments—both for domestic transactions and for international remittances. The mobile handset—with its on-the-go interactivity with the consumer—seems the ideal way to initiate such payments. Time will tell just how important these payments are to consumers beyond the current niche segments now participating.

With such a significant segment of the U.S. population in the unbanked and underbanked categories, we're watching prepaid card providers try to meet the needs of those segments with card-based payments. As card acceptance has become nearly ubiquitous (and cash,

> ### The Lure of Convenience
>
> Although convenience is probably the largest single driver of new consumer payments success, it can also be an elusive goal. Any number of unsuccessful payments start-ups have been predicated on consumer convenience—only to flounder when the actual convenience delivered fell short of the founders' vision.
>
> Early stored-value cards (with the value actually stored on a chip on the card) are a good example of this paradox. They seemed convenient at first—no cash!—but problems associated with not knowing the balance on the card, and running out of money at inopportune times, sank the consumer proposition. The smartphone seems likely to help address some of these issues.
>
> Similarly, teens—traditionally unequipped to pay with payment cards—represent another opportunity for prepaid card providers.

frankly, less so), these consumers seem to like the notion of a "bank on a card"—namely, a prepaid card. These open loop prepaid cards have been widely available, as distribution through supermarkets and other outlets has grown significantly. Reload of cash onto the cards is also widely available—further enhancing their utility.

Summary—Consumer Perspective

To summarize, consumer payments behavior is complex and influenced by many factors. Convenience and financial incentives are the most powerful drivers affecting adoption of new ways to pay. Demographic factors, while not insignificant in importance, tend to be outweighed by consumer psychographic factors. Understanding and appealing to those factors are important keys to successful consumer payments behavior change.

The Merchant Perspective

According to the 2012 U.S. economic census, there are about 5.7 million retail establishments in the U.S. market. In addition, there are about 22 million "non-employer" establishments—these range from sole proprietors, to home-office workers, to "mom and pop" retail stores. All of these, by definition, accept one or more forms of payment. From a card industry perspective, there are approximately 15 million electronic point of sale terminals that enable the acceptance of payment cards at these merchant locations.

Perhaps somewhat surprisingly, there's a high degree of concentration among the millions of merchants in the U.S. As it turns out, only some 350 major merchants are responsible for about half of all payment card transactions. Similarly, in the remote commerce world, the top 100 eRetailers account for over half of online spending.

Naturally, major merchants have more power—and options—in dealing with payments choices than do smaller "mom and pop" merchants. Indeed, the largest merchants can afford dedicated staff who deal with payments acceptance decisions, infrastructure, costs, etc.

Get Paid	Sell More	Lower Costs
Payments can play a role—direct or indirect—in all of these strategies.		
• Accept forms of payments that customers want to use • Keep/make a sale when customers are undecided or wavering	• Find new customers • Increase loyalty of existing customers • Increase customer spending power • Increase speed of checkout process	• Lower external costs of payments acceptance: fees, float, processing, risk management • Lower internal cost of transaction handling: checkout process, systems integration, training • Decrease incidents of fraud and theft

Table 8-4: Merchant Payments Motivations

Merchants Just Want to Get Paid

At the end of the day, what matters most to merchants is simply getting paid. After this, merchants look for payments solutions that will significantly increase sales. Solutions that focus on reducing costs, while important to merchants, are much less important than those that help drive higher revenues.

The introduction of the credit card offers an early example of the importance of driving higher sales. By simplifying the extension of credit to consumers, merchants who began accepting credit cards experienced higher sales, higher average tickets, and improved customer loyalty and satisfaction. Of course, there were costs involved—the "merchant discount" paid to their acquirer—but merchants were more than willing to pay in exchange for the increase in sales. After all, merchants take no credit risk on that increase; risk is handed off to the card issuer.

Of course, costs do matter to merchants when they directly affect merchant profitability—and such costs do get attention where the staff exists to deal with them. Reducing operational costs, minimizing the costs of exception handling, and negotiating lower merchant discounts are all part of the equation for major merchants seeking to reduce the cost of payments acceptance. Similarly, eliminating check acceptance and shifting consumers to debit cards lets merchants reduce credit risk, fraud risk, and associated costs.

> ### Who's a Merchant?
>
> This term comes from the card industry, which refers to all card-accepting sellers as "merchants." Many of these enterprises don't think of themselves as merchants, rather, they're "retailers," "airlines," or "phone companies," for example. In this book, we use the term to describe businesses that sell to consumers. We treat billers and enterprises serving mostly other businesses as separate classes of payments systems users.

> ### What Really Matters?
>
> Here's an important, but often overlooked, lesson in new payments adoption: We've seen a number of new product initiatives, with the value proposition of reducing merchant payments costs, flounder or fail. Meanwhile, other initiatives with a "drive merchant revenue" value proposition have succeeded. Merchants simply want to sell more!

Payments Strategies to Drive Sales and Loyalty

Over the years, merchants have embraced several extensions to basic payment card acceptance—including issuing and accepting private label cards, participating in co-branded rewards-based card programs with credit card issuers, and selling and accepting prepaid gift cards. For most merchants, these tools help drive incremental sales revenues from the broadest possible set of consumers. Merchants are also embracing the importance of convenience and speeding up payments acceptance as they consider embracing mobile payments acceptance.

The Importance of Merchant Segmentation

The importance of the cost of payments can vary significantly by merchant segment. For example, virtual goods merchants selling digital content online are much less sensitive to the cost of payments, simply because their cost of goods sold is effectively zero. For others selling hard goods at low margins, the cost of payments can become critically important. Again, segmentation is important—one size doesn't fit all when it comes to merchants' payments acceptance needs.

Remote Commerce Merchants

In the last decade, the remote commerce merchant has captured the attention of the payments industry—certainly disproportionate to the value of remote commerce when compared to physical-world commerce. This reflects a fascination with the development and potential of online commerce, but also the unique payments challenges of the remote commerce merchant.

From the early days of online retailing, virtually all remote commerce payments were made by card (credit or signature debit). Yet the cards didn't work as well for the remote commerce merchant as for the physical-world merchant.

Looking Back: eCommerce in History

Long before Amazon.com opened its virtual doors, U.S. merchants were selling to customers in what became known as "card-not-present," or CNP, environments.

These were most typically catalog sales made via mail or telephone order, and the segment became known as MOTO in the payments industry. MOTO merchants received payment both by check and by card. The card industry considered MOTO a fraud-prone segment, as the merchant could not physically see the card being presented. Because of this, MOTO transactions were not fraud-guaranteed for the merchant: if a consumer called his or her issuing bank and said "it wasn't me who ordered that," the issuing bank could credit the consumer's account and charge back the transaction to the acquiring bank, which would charge it back to the MOTO merchant's account.

When eCommerce began, the card industry simply extended this practice to online merchants. An eCommerce merchant must, therefore, manage card acceptance to avoid such fraud or to reduce it to an acceptable level. This is similar to what a physical world merchant does in accepting checks, with their risk of being bounced for insufficient funds or returned as fraudulent.

Merchant Frustrations with Payment Card Costs

Despite the benefits they receive from payment card acceptance, merchants have recently become increasingly vocal about the associated costs. Much of this frustration is the result of higher merchant discount fees charged on a new generation of rewards-based credit cards first introduced in the mid-2000's. At the time, Visa and Mastercard feared that their issuing bank partners would find the interchange-like revenue share from American Express cards more lucrative than the Visa or Mastercard interchange. In response, they issued new card types with a wide range of consumer benefits, rewards, and features—and higher interchange for issuing banks. The funding source? Higher merchant discount fees.

Merchants have responded by lobbying regulators and legislators to enact new rules that would help lower fees and by pursuing litigation against the card networks.

Other Changes in Payments Acceptance

- At the physical point of sale, merchants are replacing traditional dial-up connections with broadband—enabling faster transactions for consumers. Indeed, broadband is needed to fulfill the contactless value proposition for the consumer.

- Some merchants, particularly those who serve as everyday purchase locations, are participating in merchant-funded reward programs as they attempt to influence consumer loyalty. Though these merchants pay a higher effective merchant discount when a participating card is used, they benefit from greater customer loyalty—and thus, increased sales.

- In another effort to lower acceptance costs, some merchants are embracing ACH-based payments. By displacing card payments with ACH payments, merchants may be able to lower costs—as long as they can do so while managing the credit risk inherent in ACH.

> **MCX?**
>
> In August 2012, a group of the largest U.S. retailers announced plans to introduce a new mobile payment product, to be offered by a company called MCX (Merchant Customer Exchange). MCX will be mobile-based, merchant-centric, and low cost. Some have speculated that the formation of this group is a tactic to pressure card networks into lowering interchange. In May 2016, MCX announced it was significantly scaling back its efforts—and in March 2017 that it was selling its technology assets to JPMorgan Chase.

For several years, some merchants have been capturing check data at checkout and putting such payments through as ACH transactions, or imaging checks and depositing them electronically to their banks. These approaches offer significantly lower costs—in transaction processing and, more importantly, in the ability to represent a "bounced" check in a timely fashion.

Merchant Payments Environment

Because accepting a payment is only part of what a merchant actually does, any payments function requires some varying level of integration into the merchant's overall business environment and systems. This is another area in which segmentation is hugely important—and where endless complexity seems to reign as more and more industry-specific vendors incorporate payments functionality into their platforms.

Over the last decade, the requirements placed on merchants to ensure compliance with the Payment Card Industry-Data Security Standard (PCI-DSS) have had a significant impact on merchant systems, back-office processes, etc. Major merchants that have suffered breaches in which payment card data has been exposed have been

> **The Costs of PCI Compliance**
>
> The card industry is still grappling with the magnitude of the card data security problem—and the costs of fixing it, or at least containing its damage. Perhaps most daunting is the necessity of a high level of continued investment ("data security is a journey, not a destination"). Recent fraudster attacks have demonstrated that even PCI compliance is not enough for full protection. As a result, many merchants are considering processes to outsource payments—PaaS, or payments as a service.

hit with significant financial penalties as a result. Priority number one on many a major merchant's to-do list: ensuring PCI-DSS compliance and successfully completing an independent assessment by a third-party assessor.

The New Point of Sale

Several industry changes are underway in the U.S. market that will have large impacts on merchants and their point of sale environment.

- The U.S. historically was slow to implement the EMV chip card standard adopted by most of the rest of the world. But in 2011-2013, the card networks set a "roadmap" for EMV terminalization. This is optional for merchants, but will shift some kinds of transaction fraud liability from issuers to merchants if the merchant has not complied: for many segments of merchants, this will be a compelling reason to upgrade. EMV terminals are more expensive—but a merchant implementing EMV at this time will probably also get a terminal with contactless capabilities that supports both contactless cards as well as NFC-based mobile payments.

- Mobile payments are coming to the point of sale. After many years of experimentation, the winning technology appears to be NFC-based mobile payments. This technology makes use of the same contactless terminals that support contactless cards.

- Perhaps more significantly, merchants are being offered an even greater range of options for mobile marketing—delivering coupons and offers to a customer for redemption at the point of sale or afterwards. Many of these solutions take advantage of location-aware smartphones.

- Point of sale merchants are also dealing with other forms of mobile commerce—a consumer buying from the store using their phone, and picking up in the store; a consumer buying "in-aisle," consumer mobile self-checkout, etc.

- Finally, the onslaught of mobile card acceptance programs (Square, etc.) has crept upmarket from the original micro-merchant users, and now smartphones, or more significantly, tablets that are increasingly being used for away-from-cash-register checkout by larger merchants.

Summary—Merchant Perspective

Merchant payments acceptance practices reflect a mix of what is required by customers to effect sales and what helps a merchant increase sales and reduce costs. Because merchants can be highly vocal on the subject of payments costs, it can be tempting to overlook the critical role of payments methods in increasing sales. But even a quick look at the most successful payments innovations of the last thirty years show that their ability to increase sales has been the primary motivation in merchant adoption: credit cards (increased purchasing power); gift cards (dedicated sales); and debit cards (increased convenience and speedier checkout).

The Biller Perspective

Billers, which include utility companies, mortgage servicers, insurance companies, telecommunications and cable TV providers, the dentist, and others, are just another merchant segment. The defining characteristic of a biller, as opposed to a retailer, is the delivery or presentment of a bill to a customer. Altogether, over 100,000 billers handle about 22 billion payments per year in the U.S., in a complex acceptance environment that, again, varies by segment. Some of the segments are regulated down to the components of the bill and use of payment methods.

In general, billers need to support a broad range of consumer bill payment options. The most common consumer bill pay practice is still payment by a check sent to the biller through the U.S. mail. Increasingly, however, consumers find it more convenient to pay bills online—at either via their bank's bill payment service or on the biller's own website. Some billers accept payments via call centers or through interactive voice response (IVR); others, especially in the wireless and cable TV segments, accept payments at walk-in storefront locations.

When bills get paid also varies. Some consumers give some billers a standing instruction to deduct funds from their checking accounts or charge a particular payment card each month. Others wait until the last minute to pay—rushing to the biller's "direct" website to complete the payment and receive same-day credit for it. More traditionally, some consumers schedule mailing bill payments based on due dates. Others use banks or a third-party provider such as Western Union to make same-day rush payments, avoiding service interruption or significant late payment fees.

The tender type also varies, based on the other dimensions of bill payment. For example, use of cash makes sense only in a face-to-face payment scenario. Some billers, particularly those serving many cash-centric consumers, support walk-in bill payments primarily to facilitate taking cash. A biller wishing to take payment cards needs a traditional merchant agreement with a payment card acquirer, and with a bank for "eCheck" or ACH debit payments.

Not surprisingly, billers tend to use common practices to support the various channels and payment methods. Billers receiving large quantities of checks, for example, often use an outsourced "lockbox" to pick up the incoming mail, scan it, and receive post-process details for posting to their accounts receivable systems. The card networks have been encouraging biller-direct websites—which commonly support payment cards as their preferred payment method. Alternatively, they may support "eCheck" (ACH) payments, although more complexity and increased credit risk makes this option less attractive for some billers.

Today, biller direct is winning the online bill payment battle—having moved ahead of bank bill payment services.

Billers' Perspectives on Payments

As with merchants generally, it's important to understand that payments acceptance cost is only one consideration in terms of the biller's choice of supported payment methods. Some biller segments want consumers to come to their websites in order to cross-market new products and features while consumers are paying their bill. Others (such as mortgage servicers), for which marketing additional products makes little or no sense, are unlikely to want to spend money on a robust biller-direct website. For many billers, eliminating the operational costs of mailing paper statements is a big financial win—and PTO (paper turn off) is their holy grail. Others may decide that they want to encourage late payments, thereby driving fee income above and beyond the actual bill amount owed.

The range of biller motivations is described in the table below.

Segment	Objective	Common Strategies
All billers	Reduce statement expense	Encourage customers to come to biller's website (perhaps by accepting online credit and debit card payments)
Credit card issuers, cable, telephone billers	Cross-sell (especially credit card, telephone, cable, and online services billers)	
Utilities	Encourage customer self-service	
All billers	Lower payments acceptance costs	Use more ACH; avoid card acceptance; charge "convenience fees" for cards
Education, local tax	Comply with card network regulations	Limit "convenience fees" to online channel
Utilities	Comply with industry regulators	Use third parties to accept card payments, convenience fees go directly to third party
Mortgage processors, telephone billers, cable	Collect late payment fee revenue	Make late payments by phone or online convenient for customers; accept card payments

Table 8-5: Biller Payments Motivations

What We're Watching

The trends we're watching with respect to billers include how credit card issuers are working to educate cardholders about online bill payment and its benefits. Some banks are beginning to worry about the costs of providing online bill payment services—especially in the face of accelerated consumer adoption of biller-direct payments. Kiosk-based bill payment (enabling cash intake, for example, at unattended locations) is increasingly important for the unbanked segment. And smartphone technology seems especially useful for notifying consumers of pending bills—not to mention as a way for the consumer to actually initiate bill payment.

Summary—Biller Perspective

Each biller's perspective on payments is colored not only by considerations of cost and efficiency, but also by its other business objectives. For many biller segments, getting close to the customer is important: for cross-sales opportunities, for customer self-service, or to increase the chance of delivering statements electronically. Such billers may want to draw customers to their websites for these reasons, offering incentives (or accepting a higher cost of payments) to achieve that goal.

The Enterprise Perspective

There are more than 27 million enterprises in the United States—including businesses, nonprofit organizations, educational institutions, and local governments and agencies. The U.S. Census Bureau breaks down businesses by the number of employees; not surprisingly, these numbers are represented by a steep pyramid, with the vast majority of enterprises having 20 or fewer employees.

The merchants and billers discussed above are included in these enterprise numbers. The discussion in this section concerns enterprises other than those defined as merchants or billers.

Enterprise Payments Requirements

Even the smallest businesses have payments requirements similar to those of the largest companies. For example, businesses must control cash flow through the scheduling of payments. The ability to forecast cash inflows and outflows is fundamental to ensure the ongoing solvency and viability of an enterprise. Security and fraud risk protections are important—increasingly so as the size of the enterprise's bank accounts grow.

> **Shifting Risks**
>
> For enterprises, changes in payments systems used—at their own initiative or that of their counterparties—can bring risk management challenges. Process controls which work to manage check fraud, for example, may not apply to ACH or card transactions—which demand their own risk management processes. Also, some provisions of ACH and card network rules, and federal regulations, provide protections for consumers, but do not afford equivalent protections for enterprises.

On the cost side, businesses want to maximize the efficiency of their accounts receivables and accounts payables functions. They seek to minimize the fees they pay to banks and third parties for services, and to ensure accelerated access to good funds received.

Both large and small companies need to integrate payments data into the systems that run their companies. For small businesses, this tends to mean PC-based (or, increasingly, online) accounting packages. A larger enterprise will use one or more ERP (enterprise resource planning) systems to run its business.

Choosing Payments Providers

Decisions about what payments types to use—and which providers to choose—vary considerably by size of company.

- A very small enterprise will usually manage payments very much like a consumer does, often with the same bank used by the owner of the business.

- A medium-sized enterprise, particularly one that is growing, is often dependent on a bank or group of banks for the extension of credit. Many enterprises award basic payments business (a checking account, and check or electronic collections or disbursements) to their credit bank. A medium-sized enterprise will, as it grows, add payments providers other than the primary bank—another bank to support a regional requirement, for example, or a non-bank card acquirer or payroll processor.

- A large enterprise will treat the acquisition and management of payments services just as it does any other important business process required by the firm. A decision to select a new payments provider will often lead to the use of requests for proposals (RFPs) and a competitive bidding process. Very large enterprises have sophisticated cash management processes and complex relationships with several large banks that compete for the high-volume, lucrative payments streams of the enterprise.

Within the enterprise, checks remain the dominant form of payment, with more than 70% of large enterprise payments made via check. We've watched and waited for years for this percentage to accelerate its decline—but it stubbornly hangs in there. The check percentage for smaller enterprises is even higher; the check remains the universally convenient way to pay.

There is considerable complexity in managing the enterprise payments function in this largely paper-based payments environment. In particular, it is critically important to ensure that payments received are properly accounted for by matching them to appropriate remittance data. Similarly, to help prevent fraud, enterprises must ensure that all checks sent are securely linked to positive pay accounts. Finally, all enterprises must constantly handle exceptions—especially larger enterprises where customers may take arbitrary (so-called "self-awarded") discounts on the amount of an invoice paid, etc.

Summary—Enterprise Perspective

Most enterprises have common payments management goals: ensuring control and timing of payments, efficiency of operations, and avoidance of risk. As companies grow, the need to interact with more and more counterparties makes payments management increasingly complex.

Summary: Payments Systems Users

Payments systems users want convenience, security, and reliability in payments systems. But both consumers and merchants have complex motivations, particularly around financial incentives—both positive and negative—in using payments systems.

Perspectives on Payments: Systems Providers

THIS CHAPTER CONCLUDES A two-part look at the stakeholders that participate in any payments system. In the prior chapter, we explored the users of a payments system—in particular, the senders and receivers of the funds that flow in a payments system.

In this chapter, we look at providers of services in a payments system: banks, networks and clearing houses, and processors (which play a major behind-the-scenes role in payments systems).

The Bank Perspective

Historically, banks have owned and controlled the major payments systems in the United States. Consumers and enterprises have used the payments systems through their roles as bank customers. Banks, too, have been the primary direct economic beneficiaries of the payments system.

However, banks' status in this area has been changing, with some payments systems no longer owned by banks, and non-bank players emerging in significant roles.

Bank Segmentation

There are a lot of banks in the United States—our country undoubtedly has the highest number of banks per capita of any major country. One way of segmenting banks is by how they target consumers for retail checking account relationships. As shown in the table below, there are just three banks (as of this writing) that truly target a national market. There are hundreds, large and small, with a regional focus. And there are thousands with a local focus—including not only banks, but credit unions as well.

National	Regional	Local
Bank of America JPMorgan Chase Wells Fargo	Dozens of large regionals (U.S. Bank, SunTrust, etc.) and hundreds of smaller regional banks	8,000+ community banks 7,800+ credit unions
Not all depository institutions or all categories are listed.		

Table 9-1: Banks in the United States

Over the last few years, the banking industry has continued to consolidate, with the total number of financial institutions declining. And, as banks have increased their emphasis on online and mobile capabilities, the number of bank branch locations in the U.S. has declined—helping fuel cost savings as more expensive "brick and mortar" locations have been eliminated.

In terms of concentration based upon share of total deposits, it's still a relatively unconcentrated industry—the top three U.S. banks represent a bit over 30% of deposits (i.e., funds sitting in consumer and business checking accounts in banks, thrifts, and credit unions) with the thousands of other banks and financial institutions holding the remaining deposits.

Understanding Banks

Banks are Regulated

In the U.S., to start a bank, you need a charter from a regulatory agency—a state or federal chartering authority. The chartering authority examines the business plan, management competency, and capital adequacy of the proposed bank. The charter, when issued, defines the capabilities of the bank. The key activity is deposit taking: a non-bank can lend money or handle payments, but only a chartered institution can accept consumer deposits into a transaction account.

> **Processors Support a Broad Market**
>
> Compared to other countries, the U.S. is an unconcentrated banking market. There are many reasons for this, going back to the days when federal regulation prevented interstate banking. Today, the payments processors are one of the factors supporting an unconcentrated structure. The large processors, offering not just payments but lending, general ledger, and bank management systems, enable a single-branch or small regional bank to operate very much as if it were a division of a larger bank. Through the processors, the bank can handle checks, ACH transactions, and debit card and ATM card transactions very much as a large bank might use an in-house regional processing center.

Banks are audited and examined on an ongoing basis, often by multiple regulatory agencies; these agencies have the power to revoke a bank's charter, among other actions, if dissatisfied with its performance. The primary federal regulatory bodies in the United States are the Federal Reserve Bank, the FDIC (Federal Deposit Insurance Corporation), the OCC (Office of the Comptroller of the Currency), and the CFPB (Consumer Financial Protection Bureau). State-chartered banks are regulated by state banking authorities.

How Banks Make Money

Banks make money by lending money, by holding money (in deposit accounts or investment accounts), and by moving money—moving money means payments. Although all three activities are profitable for banks, the relative profits are highest for lending, and lending activities tend to dominate a bank's management agenda. Deposit taking is profitable on its own, but is particularly valued as a source of funds for the more profitable lending business.

Historically, payments were seen not as a line of business, but rather as an operational support function that enabled lending and deposit taking. The "productization" of the payments business has evolved within banks in fits and starts. The credit card issuing business quickly grew into a separate P&L item within most banks—a clear line of business that serves consumers. Retail checking accounts are considered a line of business in most banks; these encompass account deposits and the payments activities (checks, ATMs, debit cards, ACHs) that consumers run through accounts. Also, commercial payments accounts were offered as a free service to corporations with substantial balances at the bank. When interest rates spiked in the late 1970s and corporations began to "pull" out their bank balances for investment, this "service" evolved into today's cash management business line; banks responded by pricing payments services.

Many large and regional banks have profitable correspondent banking businesses, which provide payments services to smaller banks.

Banks are Interoperable

From the early days of check clearing houses, banks have understood the need to interoperate. Banks are sophisticated network members, and understand how consortia should be formed and managed.

Banks are Technology Savvy

Banks were early and enthusiastic adopters of new technology. Many of the routine tasks of banking, including payments processing, were well suited to automation, and the grind of the nightly "batch run"—when check payments and deposits were posted to DDA accounts—became the mainstay of bank IT managers and their mainframe suppliers. In the 1980s, banks began large-scale implementation of ATMs and, shortly thereafter, the ATM networks that grew to enable debit cards at the point of sale.

Banks were also early adopters of customer-facing online applications. Early online banking applications predated the Internet by at least a decade. Again, the simplicity of tasks involved ("check my balance"; "pay the phone company $50") was well suited to automation. Perhaps more significantly, the frequency of interaction drove bankers' interest in cost savings that could be derived from online banking.

> ### A History of Interoperability
>
> It is interesting to contrast banking with an industry such as health care in the United States. Today, hospitals and doctors are trying to figure out how to exchange electronic medical records, but the institutions do not have the history of interoperability that financial institutions (or, for another example, telecommunications firms) do, so they face a steeper learning curve.

Today, many large banks have core legacy systems for running DDAs and lending platforms that have remained largely untouched for, in some cases, decades. Banks have managed changing product, feature, and compliance requirements by wrapping ever more sophisticated layers of middleware around these core platforms.

Large banks have also become extremely adept managers of technology integration following bank mergers. Wall Street measures the efficiency of bank integration closely.

In recent years, banks have increased investment in technology to meet compliance requirements (only some of which are payments-related).

Risk Managers

Banks must, of course, be risk managers: risk management is at the heart of the lending business and is an essential component of both deposit and payments businesses. Beyond simply understanding risk and how to manage it, banks grasp the relationship between risk and profit: their most profitable businesses (most definitely including credit card issuance) demand proactive assumption of risk. Bank strategies with respect to risk management vary considerably. One credit card issuer, for example, might choose to issue cards to many consumers with relatively low credit scores, and manage performance on these accounts closely; another might choose to issue fewer cards to better customers, and give each customer a large line and more leeway.

Relationships and Products

Banks are fundamentally relationship companies: most share the strategy of trying to cross-sell multiple products to existing customers. This is true for both large and small banks, and for both consumer and commercial businesses within a bank. Many large banks measure senior managers on cross-selling success.

Banks often prioritize investments in relationship capabilities (for example, cross-bank information portals) over investments in new or enhanced product features. In fact, banks do not have a good track record on new product development. If, for example, you were to examine a list of a bank's major products today and fifty years ago, you would find very little difference in what is offered to customers—but a great deal of difference in how it is

---

The Amazing ATM

It's hard to imagine, from the standpoint of the present, just how innovative and frankly amazing the ATM was. Customers who once spent their lunch hours waiting in line to deposit a paycheck and get grocery money could now take care of business on their way home from work—or after church on Sunday.

Many bankers thought, in the early days of ATMs, that branches would eventually go away. In fact, over time, banks have learned that each new customer channel (ATMs, customer call centers, online banking, mobile banking) simply adds a new layer, without supplanting the earlier channels!

---

offered. Yesterday's checking account looks a lot like today's—but today's checking account has a debit card and ATM, online, and mobile access.

Banks and Their Challenges

Banks have a uniquely challenging relationship with their customers. Customers tend to trust their banks, but sadly, often don't like them. Consumers, in particular, have contradictory feelings about banks' stewardship of their money. They value the safety and convenience of the bank, but many are outraged at the idea that a bank might charge them for these services. It's not uncommon to hear, "It's my money—they're making money on me somehow."

Banks are also challenged by the onslaught of hundreds of "FinTech" startups that believe technology—mobile platform, data analytics, machine learning, A/B testing, etc.—can be used to develop point solutions that are far more advanced than traditional banking solutions.

Banks and Payments

Banks like the payments business for many reasons. Payments are often the reason a customer (consumer or commercial) opens an account with the bank, and are often seen as "sticky"—heavy payments users are less likely to move business to another bank. The payments business is more stable, and less risky, than the bank's lending businesses, and the revenue from the payments business (e.g., interchange or float) is often invisible to customers and, therefore, less likely to trigger problems with customer attitudes toward pricing.

Summary—Bank Perspective

The U.S. banking industry is unconcentrated, with thousands of banks needing to interoperate, particularly for payments systems. Banks value their payments businesses for the customers and revenue they bring, although they manage some payments activities as services rather than standalone products. Customer trust of banks is an asset for the payments business, but customer ambivalence about banks charging for services represents a challenge for banks.

The Paradox of Free Checking

This attitude on the part of consumers led retail bankers to develop the concept of "free checking." Free checking is free, of course, only if your balances are high enough. Retail bankers also supplement their income through bounced check and overdraft fees, and through debit card interchange—which is invisible to the consumer. The impact of the Durbin Amendment on debit card interchange for large banks eliminated an important revenue element that helped banks offer free checking.

Consumer attitudes toward the pricing of payments services make life complicated—to put it mildly—for both banks and non-bank competitors providing consumer payments services.

The Network Perspective

What is a Network?

In this section, we discuss those companies or groups that provide one or more of the three key functions of an open loop payments system: rules, brand, and processing (in particular, intermediary switching and settlement). It should be noted that there is considerable overlap between the concepts of "network" and "processor": many networks do some processing, and many processors operate transaction switches and/or own networks. Visa, for example, has a division called Visa DPS which provides issuer processing services for debit cards. Similarly, First Data Corp., one of the largest processors, also operates the STAR debit network. Closed loop payments system operators, in particular, can be thought of as both networks and processors.

Most payments networks in the U.S. began life as bank-owned consortia. Today, some remain so, while most are, or are owned by, public companies. Regardless of the ownership structure, most networks subscribe to a principle of equal treatment of members.

Network Economics and Challenges

Most networks charge for their services on a fee per transaction basis. As such, they have in common with processors the need to operate at scale to cover fixed costs, particularly of operating switching and settlement platforms. Some networks (notably Visa and Mastercard in the U.S.) also charge an ad valorem fee based on payment amount. The global card networks also derive significant revenue from cross-currency transactions that result when cardholders travel internationally.

> ### The Hand that Rules
>
> Much of the drama in the payments industry is played out in network committee rooms during rules debates. A single rule, or clause in a rule, can significantly reshape the economics of the business. For example, a decision to implement EMV chip card technology in a country will dramatically impact all of the stakeholders.

Networks tend to be volume-hungry: they actively seek new or under-penetrated markets, and compete with other payments networks for this volume.

Networks face a brand challenge: a recognizable and well-understood brand, with positive attributes associated with it, improves the networks' ability to grow volume—but sometimes can conflict with member banks' preferences that the bank brand dominate.

The biggest power of a network is its rule-making authority. In exercising this authority, the network needs to balance the loud voices of its largest users against the quieter voices of many small users. Historically, many payments systems rules were kept secret from the public, and made available only to participating members. (Famously, Visa and Mastercard used to require acquiring bank contracts to bind merchants to their rules—without letting the merchants see the rules! Today, after having become publicly traded companies, both organizations make the rules available on their websites.)

The Processor Perspective

Who are the Processors?

Every payments system involves assorted processes that must be carried out for the system to work. Sometimes these processes are simple—such as answering a customer support call. Sometimes they are complex—such as determining fraud risk in real-time. Regardless of complexity, every process can be carried out internally by employees or outsourced to a third party. When the process is outsourced to a third-party provider, that provider is referred to as a "processor."

For the purposes of this section, we define processors as:

- Companies that provide "on behalf of" transaction or account handling for banks, merchants, billers, or enterprises.

- Companies that provide private switching services for a group of banks, merchants, billers, or enterprises (but that are not included in the definition of "network" above).

- Companies that provide single—or narrow—function capabilities related to payments. This very broad category includes credit bureaus, bill pay processors, lockbox processors, security and authentication services, risk managers, collections services, and many others.

- Companies that provide hardware and/or software related to payments. This includes terminal manufacturers, card manufacturers, check stock printers, check sorters, ACH and wire transfer software processors, etc.

In the United States, along with many commercial companies that act as processors, there are two non-commercial entities that play an important role in providing processing services to banks. The Federal Reserve's Bank Payments Services organization provides check and image processing, ACH switching, wire transfer services, and cash services to banks. The Clearing House is a bank-owned enterprise that provides check image processing, ACH switching, and wire transfer services to banks. These two enterprises compete with each other, and, in some cases, with commercial providers.

Processor Challenges and Economics

Transaction handling processing is almost always a fixed-fee business (charging transaction fees, periodic maintenance fees, etc.), although there are some situations in which a processor participates in a float benefit, for example, or holds funds in escrow for a period of time. Large-scale processors often describe their business as one in which the very largest clients provide the volume for scale economies, but demand prices so low as to be virtually break-even, while the smaller clients pay higher prices that essentially provide the profit for the business model. It is not uncommon, for example, for a large processor to get over 70% of its transaction volume (measured by count or amount) from its largest clients while receiving over 50% of its revenue from its smallest clients.

Software suppliers are seeing a major shift in their business mix. Many software companies have parallel offerings—software is either licensed to a bank or merchant (and often priced on a transaction basis) or hosted at the software company; hosting can be as a dedicated application for each customer or on a shared platform. Software suppliers compete with in-house IT teams at major banks; particularly in the card business, there has been a great deal of shift as credit card issuers have consolidated.

Payments Services Providers

A special category of non-bank payments providers we call "payments services providers" serve end parties directly. Consumer-facing payments services providers include check cashing companies, bill payment companies, prepaid card issuers, and money transfer services (such as Western Union and MoneyGram). There are also consumer and merchant-facing payments services providers, particularly in the eCommerce domain—PayPal, Google, etc. Definitions here are slippery, of course: one could categorize closed loop card networks (such as American Express historically) and merchants offering private-label credit, debit, or prepaid cards as being "payments services providers," as well.

Payments services providers must invest in the brand and market channels necessary to reach their end parties directly. They may provide processing (transaction handling, account opening, customer service) themselves, or contract with other processors to provide it. If such providers are funding payment transactions from other payment accounts (for example, from credit cards, debit cards, or direct access to bank accounts), they typically make arrangements with one or more banks that are members of the necessary networks. Similarly, if they are handling outbound payments through established networks, they need to make arrangements for this.

Many payments services providers handle cross-border payments; to do so, they may establish private networks of banks (which have correspondent relationships with each other) to process and clear transactions. Payments services providers may, over time, develop significant "on-us" volumes, and can process these transactions internally, without relying on external banks or networks.

The economic models of payments services providers are usually complex, and reflect a mix of direct revenues from end parties (merchant discount fees or consumer fees, for example) and indirect revenues from float, foreign exchange fees, and, in certain situations, interchange fees shared by a bank partner. In addition to the routine expenses of managing their business, payments services providers usually assume some degree of risk in handling transactions, and must invest in the capability to manage acceptable levels.

Summary: Payments Systems Providers

Providers play many different roles in payments systems. Some roles are infrastructural—deep in the plumbing of the systems. These providers offer intermediary switching, processing, or supporting services, and are often invisible to the end parties to a transaction. Other providers are highly visible to both consumers and merchants. Many providers, including banks, processors, networks, and payments services providers, play roles that encompass both infrastructural and customer-facing elements. Providers in the payments industry face challenges in acquiring the scale necessary for cost-efficient processing. Higher margins often accrue more to those providers able to charge ad valorem, or a percentage of the dollar value of transactions processed, than to those charging flat fees for transaction processing.

Payments Innovation

"My general analysis of my PayPal experience is that if I knew everything I know now about the payments space, I never would have started the company."
— Peter Thiel, co-founder/former CEO, PayPal

Introduction

At Glenbrook, we're excited to see innovation in payments. Having our "roots" in Silicon Valley offers us a unique vantage point from which we can interact face-to-face with entrepreneurs embarking on their path to try to change the world and with the venture investors who finance them.

We carefully follow the news every day as it relates to payments, commerce, and related technologies. We share what we find interesting on our PaymentsNews.com daily news blog and frequently highlight for our clients' attention those news items we suspect might affect their businesses in the future.

As a result, we evaluate many new payments concepts and companies—often for our clients, and sometimes just to educate ourselves. We also forecast markets and make predictions about the likelihood of success of particular innovations. Sometimes we're right and sometimes we're wrong—but we think we're right more often than not!

Still, we're humbled anytime we miss new markets or ideas and, along with others, have to play catch-up! (What's an example of what we've missed? The emergence of a third-party distribution model in prepaid cards—which led to the success of companies like Blackhawk Network and InComm, among others.) We're always seeking to understand new payments innovations—whether based on changes in technologies, business models, regulatory environment, marketing, etc.—that we haven't yet seen or anticipated.

When we began offering our Payments Boot Camp—a two day "deep dive" into the U.S. payments industry—in the summer of 2005, we primarily focused on the basics of the five core payments systems in the U.S., how users use them to make payments, and how the providers and infrastructure make everything work. We spent very little time describing how those systems might evolve.

We soon realized however that, while focusing on the basics was useful for our attendees, most of them were also keenly interested in our perspectives on how these systems might evolve based on the rapid pace of technology innovation already well underway. Since those early years over a decade ago, we've significantly enhanced the Payments Boot Camp to address those interests. We now spend almost the entire second day of each session on the topics of emerging payments technologies and payments innovation. And, as the industry continues to evolve, we update the content constantly in order to keep pace with the ongoing changes in the industry. To date, we've educated more than 14,000 payments professionals in our public and private Payments Boot Camps and workshops.

Because of this pace of continuous change, we dealt very briefly with emerging payments and innovation in the first two editions of this book. In this edition, we attempt a more comprehensive examination of the topic—as we describe some of the more important lessons learned from payments innovations over the last decade.

Finally, we also examine some of the most important shifts in technologies and culture that may lead to future innovations. We hope that this more extended treatment provides a more suitable capstone to our study of payments systems in the U.S.—and we welcome your comments and feedback!

The Nature of Change

The world of payments innovation encompasses both evolutionary and, much less frequently, revolutionary changes to the ways that payments happen. As we've followed the industry for over thirty years, we've seen many examples of evolutionary innovation—these are the kinds of innovation that industry incumbents introduce as they refine their product and service offerings to serve their largest and best customers.

The evolution of card technology from magnetic stripe to EMV chip cards is an example of an evolutionary change by the card networks. The introduction of PCI-DSS data security standards is another example. Defining acceptance rules that support purchases in non-face-to-face environments is yet another. As incumbents listen to their best customers and define new enhancements to serve them better, they're pursuing evolutionary innovation.

Revolutionary innovation, on the other hand, rarely happens in these environments.

In contrast to evolutionary innovations, revolutionary innovations typically come from the small seedlings in the rainforest of big trees. These new entrants are free to innovate unburdened by having existing customers. They can work at applying new technologies in combination with new business insights to pursue an emerging market opportunity. Only a few, however, will gain enough of a foothold to actually achieve some measure of success.

Achieving success with a revolutionary innovation isn't easy or simple. It's hard work. Peter Thiel, co-founder and CEO of PayPal, has said, "My general analysis of my PayPal experience is that if I knew everything I know now about the payments space, I never would have started the company. It would be too intimidating."

Thiel's comment illustrates another characteristic often found when successful revolutionary innovation occurs: namely, that the successful revolutionaries aren't from within the industry. They have the benefit of being unencumbered by the so-called common wisdom within an industry. This provides them the freedom to challenge that wisdom (or dogma!) in new ways.

Revolutionary innovations often "enter from below" in the classic "innovator's dilemma" fashion. The new entrant begins by serving customers that, for whatever reason, aren't being served by industry incumbents. Those incumbents tend to minimize the significance of the new entrant since it's not attacking the incumbents' best customers. In fact, incumbents often feel that the new entrant has no chance of succeeding—since it doesn't offer a product or service that would be compelling to the incumbents' existing customers. This attitude on the part of the incumbents provides space for the new entrant to expand—to the point where the new entrant may eventually have developed a stronger value proposition that does appeal to the incumbents' best customers. The risk for the incumbents is that their ability to respond may be limited at that point.

Executives in industry incumbent companies should always question comments from people within their organizations that disparage a new entrant's potential ability to succeed. That form of organizational arrogance creates blind spots that result in ignoring revolutionary innovations that just might succeed!

The Job to be Done

When considering developing new approaches to solving problems, it's important to avoid being swept away by the power of a particular new technology or a radical new business model. On the other hand, it's also important to consider how these innovations can enable change and, occasionally, help enable a successful new market entry. A focus on the job to be done is critical to matching solutions to market needs.

Steve Ellis, head of innovation at Wells Fargo Bank, puts it this way: "Customers don't want disruption, they want new kinds of value that make life easier for them." In other words, the customer has a job that needs doing and is simply looking for the easiest and most convenient way to get it done.

The notion of "jobs to be done" has emerged as an important consideration for assessing what's important when innovating. The core notion of this approach, as described by Professor Clayton M. Christensen at the Harvard Business School, is to step back from the solution itself to consider what, exactly, is the customer trying to accomplish—what's the job she's looking to "hire" a new solution to accomplish?

Asking this question helps ensure that the focus of innovation is on the customer's real need and not just on what the new entrant has available to sell. Frankly, this notion sounds almost too obvious or basic—but we've watched many entrepreneurs over the years become so enamored with their solutions that they risk losing sight of the job the customer is trying to do.

While there are many different forms of payments, the basic job to be done is simple—provide an exchange of value from buyer to seller. Solutions that are unencumbered with excess features and can deliver very convenient payments experiences are the goal. Someone once said, "Seek simplicity and distrust it"—another useful mantra to consider when innovating in payments. Finding the right combination of new technologies offering new capabilities, coupled with innovative business models is tough—but can be very successful if the powerful network effects of two-sided adoption kick in.

For example, consider the job to be done when you need to pay for dinner at a local restaurant. You could choose to pay with cash—or you could choose to pay with a credit or a debit card. The job is simple, but multiple technologies are available to you to help complete the task. As we've discussed earlier in this book, you'll likely be motivated to choose the solution that provides the best "fit" for your needs—in terms of convenience and the potential for financial rewards. The card issuer that's equipped you with the card (or mobile payment option) best matching those attributes will likely be the one that you choose.

On the other hand, if you're making a purchase online, the job to be done changes—you still simply need to move money to the seller—but the available tools change. No longer is cash an option—it simply doesn't work for non-face-to-face payments. Payments with cards become less convenient as you need to remember and type in the card details that were automatically read in the restaurant example. These elements of friction provide an opening for introducing a better solution to the job to be done—one that PayPal took early advantage of by simplifying the online checkout process and eliminating the need for the buyer to provide their card details for every purchase.

As another example, let's consider what the job to be done is for a payments network like Visa. Networks primarily serve their bank issuer partners and, secondarily, their bank acquirers and their merchant customers. The jobs the issuers hire the network to do include providing the system structure and rules that facilitate the exchange of value. Other jobs that issuers hire networks to do include ensuring widespread acceptance to maximize customer utility, as well as managing the integrity of the network to minimize risks and fraud. Bank issuers, on the other hand, aren't hiring the network to market their card products to potential customers. Nor are the issuers hiring the network to manage credit issuance or collections from cardholders.

PayPal provides another illustration of focusing on a job to be done. After several early attempts at identifying a market, PayPal was drawn into supporting small sellers on the auction site, eBay, who were not well served by any payments solutions available from industry incumbents. Traditional merchant card acquirers would not underwrite these small sellers so they were unable to accept card payments from buyers—that was the job they needed done. PayPal's initial success was providing these small sellers with a simple means to accept card payments. In so doing, PayPal took a revolutionary approach to underwriting these small sellers. It successfully innovated by bringing together both technology and business model elements that led to its early success with this formerly unserved market of small sellers.

A final example of focusing on a job to be done in payments is provided by Square. Frustrated by a friend's experience as a craft merchant who missed a sale because he couldn't take credit cards, Jack Dorsey and his founding team at Square recognized the potential to enable smartphones, with wide area network connectivity and availability, to be used as credit card accepting devices. But the mobile technology they brought to bear to enable this job to be done was only part of the solution. Square also needed to make it super simple for a small seller to be approved for payments acceptance. In combination, they delivered a combination of innovations that helped further expand card acceptance and reduced the need for cash.

Ensuring clarity of focus on the "jobs to be done" helps ensure the most appropriate alignment between customer and provider. It may seem basic, but there are many examples of failed initiatives that neglected to take heed of the requirements of the job to be done.

Where Innovation Happens

As discussed earlier in this book, we like to think of payments as being comprised of three steps that transfer value from sender to receiver: initiation of the payment, funding of the payment (by the sender) and settlement of the payment (with the receiver). These steps are shown in the diagram below.

Every payment transaction must be initiated, funded, and completed. The relative timing of these processes can vary by system and type of provider.

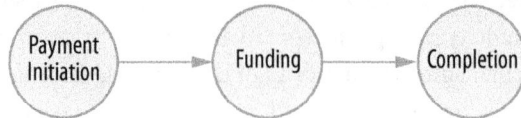

Figure 10-1: A Simple Payments Value Chain

For example, in a credit card purchase transaction at a physical point of sale location, the cardholder initiates the transaction by providing his payment card—containing the required card credentials—to the merchant or the merchant's point of sale terminal. Once the card information is captured, the transaction is authorized by the card issuer—which provides a guarantee that the funds are available in the consumer's account or credit line. Finally, the merchant submits the transaction details through the merchant's acquirer and receives settlement of funds after the acquirer has settled and received funds from the card network on the merchant's behalf.

When we examine successful innovations in payments, we find that many of the innovations begin with a focus on the initiation step, while not attempting to change the other two steps. Where only payments initiation changes are involved, we may not think of them as being very innovative. For example, a contactless card transaction uses different technology to read the physical card but the underlying way the transaction is funded (as either a debit card or credit card) and how payment to the merchant is completed is unchanged.

Similarly, PayPal began using email addresses and passwords to initiate payments—replacing the use of 16-digit card numbers and expiration dates. The rest of PayPal's early transactions rode the card network rails for payment funding and completion. Only later did PayPal take the next step to innovate with respect to the funding step—adding the option for funding directly from the buyer's bank checking account in lieu of payment cards. In the process, PayPal benefited from an important change in the economics of its business. Funding directly from the buyer's checking account was considerably cheaper for PayPal than using credit/debit card funding. Interestingly, the ability for PayPal to use this alternative funding approach came about as the result of a rule change that enabled a new type of ACH transaction—the WEB transaction.

Sometimes we may also see a "doubling up" where a payments service replaces a single payment transaction with two transactions behind the scenes. PayPal's use of card or ACH funding is an example. PayPal conducts one transaction between its buyer and seller—using a separate funding transaction to go get the buyer's funds from the buyer's card or checking account via ACH. We describe these kinds of transactions as "decoupled transactions"— a single transaction actually decomposing into two separate transactions in different payments systems.

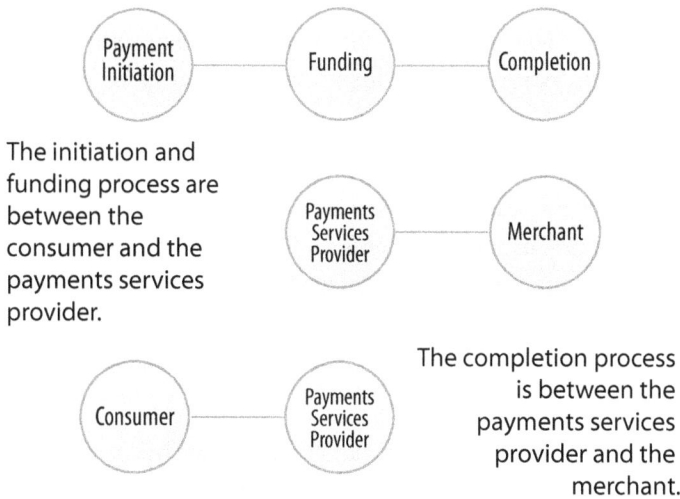

Figure 10-2: Doubling Up Payments

In these situations, an important part of the innovation is providing a seamless wrapper around the payment experience—from the perspectives of the buyer and seller—even as multiple payment systems may be involved "under the covers." In spite of how the "plumbing" is actually constructed, it remains the responsibility of the innovator to be clear in branding and marketing the solution if adoption is going to ultimately succeed.

The Payments Innovation Challenge

Payments innovations involve either unilateral change—where only the sender or receiver is affected by the innovation—or they involve bilateral change that affects both the sender and the receiver. There is a significantly higher degree of difficulty when both parties are required to change to adopt a new payment innovation. It's much easier to gain adoption if only one party is required to change.

Obviously, the nature of the innovation determines whether it will require change by one or both parties. Successful innovators think carefully about this and seek to avoid the complexity of bilateral adoption by both parties, if possible. But sometimes bilateral adoption is actually what's required.

This notion of bilateral adoption is perhaps the most challenging aspect for payments innovators. If both parties are required to be involved, the innovator has to demonstrate a meaningful benefit to both sides to incent their adoption. This can be very challenging, especially in the early days.

Merchants, for example, aren't interested in adopting some new payments innovation unless it brings them meaningful value—including having an understanding that their customers want them to embrace the new innovation and implement it where required. Similarly, consumers aren't interested in adopting an innovation if it has limited utility in terms of where they can use it.

Gift cards provide a useful example of unilateral change. When introduced in the mid-1990's as a replacement for the traditional paper gift certificate, merchant acquirers brought gift cards to their merchant customers who embraced them. There was no requirement for other parties to be involved—the merchant's acquirer could provide the whole program to the merchant. Quickly, over a couple of years, all major merchants worked with their acquirers to implement gift cards.

Another great example of successful unilateral change has been the Starbucks prepaid card and mobile application. Once again, only Starbucks needed to be involved in enabling this unilateral change. Consumers could both acquire and use Starbucks cards at their local store—without the involvement of any other payments ecosystem player. When smartphone-based mobile applications became available, Starbucks took early advantage to enable their customers to pay—and, ultimately, both order ahead and pay—using their Starbucks mobile app. The high frequency of repeat visits by regular Starbucks customers visiting multiple times each week helped accelerate adoption of Starbucks mobile payments app—resulting in Starbucks being far and away the first major success story in mobile payments in the U.S.

Square provides examples of both success and failure in this regard. Square's one-sided merchant mobile POS card acceptance offering proved to be a big success—enabling small merchants to equip themselves for card acceptance without requiring their customers to change anything. On the other hand, Square also tried innovating with several ideas that did require consumer-side adoption including the Square Wallet. This app connected the consumer's smartphone with the merchant's Square Register in an attempt to make the payment more convenient. Not surprisingly, Square Wallet failed to gain any meaningful consumer adoption and was ultimately shut down.

Building Blocks for Payments Innovation

Innovations emerge when innovators combine the right set of building blocks to address the most important jobs to be done.

A building block can be a new or improved technology that makes possible something new that previously wasn't possible. Or, a building block may be a new business approach—perhaps enabled by the regulatory environment, legislation, or even payment network rule changes.

The ongoing development and evolution of technology has helped fuel many of the innovations in payments. While the effects of new technologies have been impressive, it's also the combination of technology with new ways to think about payments—including business "rules" and financial regulation—that's helped enable change.

In this section we'll explore both the new technologies and the new business approaches that might further combine to deliver new payments innovations.

Building Blocks—Technologies

All of the modern payments systems—beyond cash—rely on the power of computers and communications networks to operate. Even cash, while considered primarily a tactile paper and coin-based system, relies on computers and communications to provide distribution of cash (ATMs) and for anticounterfeit technologies.

As computer and communications technologies have evolved over the last decade, we've seen an impressive increase in performance making a dramatic difference in the kinds of problems that computers can address. A corresponding dramatic reduction in the size and power requirements of computer chips has been an equally important part of this evolution.

But it's the combination of this progress in computing technologies, coupled with an even more dramatic improvement in communications technologies, that's fueled much of the progress in technology. Harnessed within the smartphone, these technologies have provided billions of people on the planet the equivalent of a "supercomputer in their pocket"—one which is also capable of connecting with every other smartphone on the planet over a high-speed, resilient communications network—actually, multiple networks.

As I (Scott) am writing this chapter, I'm working comfortably at a desk in a public library in Palo Alto, California—using an Apple iPad Pro that's connected to the Internet over a delightfully fast Wi-Fi network provided by the library. I'm running on the battery in the iPad that provides me with enough power to work all day without making a power connection. I'm using Microsoft Word to write this document, which automatically saves each change I make to my cloud storage account. I can review and markup PDFs or make illustrations using my Apple Pencil on the screen of the iPad. I can take very high quality pictures with the camera. Helping me stay engaged, I can listen to music in my headphones as I work. Should I take a break to walk outside and down the block to a café, my iPad will switch from the library's local Wi-Fi network to AT&T's LTE high-speed cellular network—enabling me to continue my research and writing as I move locations. My iPad Pro uses biometric authentication of my fingerprint to provide convenient and secure access. I can also store my credit or debit card details securely on the device and then make payments in applications using Apple Pay. This is an amazingly powerful combination of computer and communications capabilities now in my hands. We have every expectation that this will continue to improve incrementally—and, perhaps, even in a revolutionary fashion.

The ever increasing performance of these devices helps make possible whole new application ideas based on the use of the "cloud"—with computing, storage, machine learning, and other resources working on remote services in tandem with the applications on our mobile devices. This is a powerful combination and provides a new paradigm for building applications and services we can barely imagine today. We are following several technologies and trends that are likely to help accelerate payments innovation in the future.

These technologies—all potential building blocks for payments innovation—include:

- **The "cloud":** Over the last decade, the emergence of cloud-based services has radically shifted the economics of what's possible for young companies to pursue. New services such as Amazon Web Services, Google Cloud Platform, Microsoft Cloud, etc. allow web-based businesses to create new services and applications online without the investment in hardware and software previously required—substantially reducing the amount of capital that must be raised to get initial product offerings to market.

- **APIs:** Building upon the capabilities of open communications networks and cloud-based access to services, companies can create APIs (application programming interfaces) that allow new services to be created which rely upon existing services for part of their solution. API architectures enable these to be constructed in ways that ensure the integrity of the solution, using sophisticated authentication techniques to ensure appropriately managed access in a very efficient manner. Increasingly, incumbents are enabling API access to many of their services and capabilities, as they seek to transform their role into one of providing a "platform" upon which young companies can build and innovate while the incumbent remains at the center in terms of their role.

- **App stores:** Similar to the cloud, the availability of app stores has significantly eased the distribution challenges previously faced by young companies. For example, the Apple App Stores (for iOS and Macintosh) and Google Play (for Android) enable developers to publish and distribute new applications very quickly—and to derive revenue from those applications without concerning themselves with how to accept payments in countries around the world. These app stores can also be used to distribute free applications which provide mobile extensions to core functions—such as mobile banking applications, and mobile ordering and payments for merchants such as Chipotle, Starbucks, etc.

- **Open source software:** Another important technology shift over the last twenty years has been the rapid growth in the availability of open source software that can be used as the foundation for many new applications and services. Freely available open source packages allow young companies to compress their development cycles to rapidly implement their ideas. They also provide the mechanism whereby any enhancements can be shared back with the open source community to further enhance the core foundations—providing a very powerful innovation feedback loop. This also now extends to recruiting talent— with contributions to open source software projects now considered important evidence of an engineer's capabilities.

- **Big data, machine learning, and artificial intelligence:** The ability to store and analyze massive amounts of data is another important technology shift. These technologies provide the means to evaluate and understand patterns that can be used to build machine intelligence that analyzes new events as they occur. The card industry has used similar technologies for over 25 years to look for suspicious transactions and to identify points of compromise where card data may have been surreptitiously acquired. Recent advances in these fields are enabling new insights to be derived from massive amounts of data, which is likely to lead to new applications for both risk reduction and marketing applications related to payments. We've already seen the emergence of so-called "robo-advisors" in personal financial management and can anticipate new payments innovations based on these technologies.

- **Voice interfaces:** Over the last five years, voice interaction with computers has emerged as the next generation human interface—the next step beyond keyboards and text. Examples include the introduction of Amazon Echo, Apple's Siri, and Google Now, which respond to our voice commands and provide voice responses to our queries or instructions. While still in the early days, we expect rapid progress will occur in this area including the use of voice biometric authentication to verify users for access to services. Amazon's Echo, for example, allows voice ordering of certain items—including re-ordering previously ordered items from Amazon, as well as making it easy to add items to a shopping list. Capital One is already using Amazon Echo to support customer service inquiries such as inquiring about your current account balance, reporting on recent transactions, and even paying your credit card bill. Square is using Siri voice commands on the iPhone to initiate Square Cash payments.

- **Wearables:** Clearly smartphones have had a dramatic impact on us over the last decade. We're now just beginning to see the introduction of wearable devices such as the Apple Watch that further extend the capabilities of mobile devices. The Apple Watch supports Apple Pay—making it easier to pay at the POS without having to find and use either your payment card or your smartphone. We expect the power and utility of these kinds of wearable devices will accelerate and become another platform on which we will conduct commerce and make payments.

- **Virtual Currencies:** The emergence of new forms of cryptography-based currencies, such as Bitcoin, has drawn a lot of interest, both positive and negative. Admirers cheer the potential for a globally usable currency that might augment today's approach to cross-border payments that is based upon a network of correspondent banking relationships. Skeptics question how anyone could put their faith in a scheme that lacks any central ownership or management.

- **Blockchain:** Looking beyond Bitcoin, many admire the notion of the Blockchain—a new shared database structure that could make more efficient certain financial services use cases. We also see examples emerging such as Open Bazaar and its use of the Blockchain to create peer-to-peer marketplaces that enable trading without any central authority. An area of considerable investor interest over the last several years, we expect to continue to see surprising innovations affecting payments and financial services come out of this sector.

- **Invisible payments:** Sometimes it's the removal of complexity that yields better, more simplified results. One example of this is how Uber handles payments for its ride sharing service. Uber completely removes the payment interaction by handling it automatically at the conclusion of the ride. The payment still happens—but the consumer need not concern himself at the destination and can simply get out of the car. It's reminiscent of Amazon's 1-Click payment, an early innovation that made purchasing on Amazon.com simple and easy. We expect we'll see other examples of this kind of simplicity from other innovators.

- **Platform payments:** The Internet has affected us in so many ways —including how it has enabled new business models that require new payments solutions. The emergence of "marketplaces" has driven the need for payments solutions that don't simply involve a sender and a receiver of funds. Marketplaces have a third party—the marketplace operator—that is involved as a platform operator between buyers and sellers. Companies like Uber, Airbnb, Etsy, and Kickstarter provide platforms that connect sellers with potential buyers—facilitating all manner of commerce from ride sharing to room rentals to crowd funding and more. Traditional payment solutions aren't always appropriate for these kinds of platform-centric businesses. New entrants, including companies like WePay, have emerged to focus on these kinds of businesses and their payments needs. We expect to see continued growth in these kinds of platform companies with innovators emerging who help them with payments and more.

- **Data security:** Protecting the integrity of payments systems is obviously core to ensuring trust and confidence in those systems. Data breaches that compromise payment card data erode that confidence. Similarly, hacking events that compromise access to global payments systems are at least as concerning. Core to the successful use of any of the technologies we're discussing here will be the ability to use them in safe and secure manners that prevent unauthorized access and abuse. Successful payments innovators will pay appropriate attention to these issues—they've become "table stakes" for payments innovation.

The combined effects of these technologies will fuel an accelerated pace of innovation globally as old barriers to entry are replaced by new approaches that enable rapid innovation at scale. We also expect that, while this list of technology building blocks is already lengthy, we'll learn of other new technologies that will also prove to be important to payments innovation in the future.

Building Blocks—Beyond Mobile

The last decade of evolution in mobile technologies and services has had a dramatic impact on each of us. The pace of smartphone evolution has been extreme—and the global involvement of third-party application developers has brought a seemingly endless array of mobile-based services to our handsets. But what lies ahead? Can this pace continue or will we witness other changes we've not yet imagined?

In the Google 2016 Founders' Letter, CEO Sundar Pichai focused his discussion around the power of machine learning and artificial intelligence (AI)—not on mobile devices. He wrote:

> "Looking to the future, the next big step will be for the very concept of the 'device' to fade away. Over time, the computer itself—whatever its form factor—will be an intelligent assistant helping you through your day. *We will move from mobile first to an AI first world.*"

As discussed earlier as a technology building block, the use of voice interfaces—with us talking to our devices—is already happening and seems to represent the next generation user interface that will simply become part of how we live and work.

How will machine learning and AI affect the worlds of payments? Will we be able to efficiently detect, and essentially eliminate, fraud in payments—and what are the implications if so?

Will we talk to our financial institutions as "bots" in Facebook Messenger—effectively programming them to watch, react, and notify on our behalf?

In the rapidly emerging world of the Internet of Things, will the fabric of value exchange be fundamentally different—based on push payments among machines who have jobs to be done that other machines can fulfill? What will be the human implications of these kinds of changes—will jobs be created or destroyed?

One thing is very clear: the power to analyze vast amounts of information and to derive new insights from it is already here. The custodianship of vast data resources, coupled with the cloud-based infrastructures for rich analysis and machine learning, will have major implications for how financial services companies will evolve.

Building Blocks—New Business Approaches

The use of new technologies has helped fuel new business approaches that further extend the impact of technologies on the world of payments.

For example, the addition of a computer chip to a traditional credit card—now known more familiarly as an EMV chip—was made possible by the evolution of computer silicon chips small enough and cheap enough to enable use in very large quantities on cards to thwart counterfeiting of card credentials. While the simple magnetic stripe was an important innovation fifty years ago that enabled the information encoded on cards to be quickly and cheaply read by merchant point of sale readers, it was also trivially easy for fraudsters to copy and create cloned counterfeit cards which would work just as well as the original.

What was needed to combat that form of card fraud was new technology that would allow a deeper verification of the card's legitimacy at time of use. The EMV chip became that solution—as the result of a major cross-industry collaboration effort by the card companies to agree on a common use and the technical standards to make EMV cards interoperable. Business rules were then defined to help drive implementation of new POS readers capable of handling the EMV chips. This combination of new technology and a new business approach defined the solution.

An important change in business approach occurred when the former bank-owned association structures of Visa and Mastercard evolved to become publicly traded companies. In doing so, their boards of directors had to evolve from being all bankers to being directors representing the interests of the companies' new public shareholders. In the process, the networks—now more appropriately called "card companies"—have evolved, from relatively rigid regulatory regimes based on operating rules and regulations, to participating more actively in innovation. PayPal is an example of this. PayPal emerged as a new solution to online payments for online auctions. Instead of demanding strict compliance with operating rules that might have limited the growth of PayPal, Visa and Mastercard separately crafted new rules that clarified how the new entrant (and similar companies) could operate successfully using the cards of both networks.

PayPal provides another example of a new business approach enabling a new solution also involved PayPal. In order to enable "instant payments" on the PayPal platform, PayPal needed to implement what has been called a "decoupled" transaction approach. In this approach, PayPal provides the appearance of a sender's funds arriving instantaneously in the receiver's account even though the transaction may actually be funded using the sender's credit card—using a system providing funding on a next business day cycle. PayPal found it to its advantage to offer this instant payment capability, built the systems, and designed its own set of operating rules to bring together disparate systems to provide the solution.

A more recent innovation in card payments has been the development of prepaid cards. These cards don't involve the use of any new technologies—rather, new business rules created the opportunities for prepaid cards. All of the card companies have embraced these cards—which allow card issuance to the broad base of consumers without requiring the cost and, importantly, the qualification of new cardholders for credit, or requiring that they have a bank checking account.

As discussed earlier, prepaid cards initially entered the market as a single-sided innovation replacing gift certificates at merchants. Merchant acquirers saw the opportunity to migrate merchant gift certificates from the old paper-based approach that involved a totally manual process to a new, card-based approach that automated the whole process.

Later, further innovation in the prepaid card industry occurred when third-parties discovered the opportunity to act as distributors for these cards—stocking them in the checkout lanes at supermarkets, for example, and making them very easy for consumers to buy either for themselves or to give as gifts. Blackhawk Network and InComm are perhaps the two best examples of these companies. To enable the sale and immediate activation of prepaid cards, these companies built the technology platforms to interconnect to the sellers' POS systems—enabling a consumer to buy (and load) a prepaid card and then immediately walk to a store next door and use it. Both the rules defining prepaid cards and the distribution/integration technologies were required for success.

It's the combination of new technologies and new business approaches that lead to successful payments innovation. Often incumbents in the industry can put the right combination of these two ingredients together and introduce an evolutionary innovation. Sometimes, more rarely, new entrants can see a different combination that challenges the status quo. There's been a lot of "road kill" on the payments innovation highway—but those who can break through can be very successful.

Regulatory Influence

A final but important influence on payments innovation is the influence of regulators—and enabling legislation that provides regulators with oversight authority. These influences vary dramatically from country to country—but they establish the fundamental ground rules within which payments innovators must operate.

Recent examples of regulatory influence in several countries relate to faster payments initiatives—as regulators press for the implementation of new faster payments systems even as the banking industry may question the market requirements for these systems as they worry about the potential impact on their existing revenue streams. In the U.S., the Federal Reserve has embarked on an initiative to study this area.

Beyond Payments to Commerce

Over the last decade, we've experienced great deal of innovation—successful and unsuccessful—in payments. Increasingly, we sense the importance of taking a step back from just the payments job to be done—to also focus on the commerce aspects. Merchants seek to drive revenue through successful sales.

Success is much more than just handling payments—it's all about driving awareness and helping lead a buyer from prospect to customer.

Payments play an important role in concluding the purchase—and may help in the earlier stages where innovators broaden the scope of their approach. We expect to see the combination of commerce and payments to be an important focus for innovation.

Beyond the U.S.

While this book is focused on payments systems in the United States, any discussion about payments innovation must include some discussion about the innovation occurring in countries outside the U.S.

One of the powerful effects of the global Internet is its reach—enabling innovators to explore and invent on a global stage. That said, payments systems are, by definition, primarily national in scope, with important differences between and among payments systems in different countries. These differences can be the sources of new opportunities—we might be almost blind to those opportunities here in the U.S. while they might be very significant elsewhere.

Examples include the emergence of person-to-person payments systems such as M-Pesa in Kenya. These systems address market requirements in an innovative new way that simply wouldn't work in the U.S.

Similarly, in India, the government's focus on biometric authentication for all citizens is providing an important foundation layer for accelerating financial inclusion in the country.

Savvy entrepreneurs will pay attention to these national differences that create new areas for innovation in those countries that may also end up being relevant at some point in the U.S.

Achieving Success in Payments Innovation

With this background on the technology and business building blocks available for payments innovation, we now turn to some of the lessons learned about successful payments innovations.

We've had many interactions over the years with entrepreneurs pursuing their dreams for innovation in payments—and we've had a unique vantage point from which to both assist with and learn from their experiences. We've distilled our observations about the most important factors down to these:

1. Solve the Chicken-and-Egg Problem

As discussed earlier, a payments system needs to provide compelling benefits for both the payer and the payee. In addition (to use a consumer purchase example), it must have enough merchants on board to interest consumers, and enough consumers on board to interest merchants. Therein lies the biggest challenge for successful adoption of a payments innovation that requires bilateral adoption.

2. Get the Economic Model Right

It's not always obvious in payments who the paying customer is. Is it the payer or the payee? Both? Neither? Are the charges visible or invisible, to one or both end parties? Is there an ad valorem (percentage of value) component? What are the risks—and how is risk distributed and priced?

The cost of customer acquisition is another critical factor and may dominate the early stage expenses of a new entrant. Credit card industry veterans are very familiar with this having observed the multi-million dollars of cost spent to introduce the Discover Card to the market in the 1980's.

More recently, with the advent of much lower distribution costs enabled by the Internet, new entrants have successfully used "viral marketing" strategies to help drive customer acquisition. PayPal is perhaps the best example of using "bounties" to incent their users to invite their friends to sign up—and, in the process, rewarding both parties with a $10 credit.

3. Understand How to Operate in Scale

Payments systems that are successful tend to get very big, very fast. At the beginning, establishing a reputation for trust and integrity is critical—it's very difficult for a payment service to become successful if it's launched "in beta."

Trust, confidence, and reliability are core to the value proposition of a payments system—they are required—and the supporting systems infrastructure must be designed with those requirements in mind. These requirements will further burden the expense side of the profit and loss statement of a new entrant—further complicating the challenge of getting to break-even and, ultimately, to profitability.

4. *Understand the Regulatory Requirements*

In the early years of the Internet, new payments startups frequently did not understand the regulatory environment and how they might run afoul of various regulatory obligations that apply to companies that receive or transmit funds on behalf of others. For example, PayPal encountered objections from state regulators who intervened during their initial public offering.

Another challenge in the regulatory arena in the U.S. is the state vs. federal level regulatory regimes. Regulatory changes are also an ongoing challenge and obtaining appropriate licensing can be both time consuming and costly for new entrants. Seeking the counsel of experienced banking regulatory attorneys is another significant requirement that must be incorporated into the business plan for any new entrant.

To make matters even more challenging, these regulatory requirements vary significantly in other countries beyond the U.S. Each market must be considered uniquely and compliance addressed appropriately for each country in which the new entrant seeks to operate.

Summary: Payments Innovation

In this chapter we've shared what we've learned from observing and working with innovators in payments. The pace of progress has been robust, yet we feel we are on the brink of even more rapid innovation ahead.

We're awash in new technologies with potential application to payments and commerce. There's a global workforce of entrepreneurs and skilled engineers able to bring new solutions to market.

Many entrants, indeed most based on history, are likely to struggle and stumble—but we know there will be important successes that emerge and achieve market success. We look forward to being with them as they embark on their journeys!

Appendix

Industry Terminology/Acronyms

Term	Definition	Payment System
A2A	Account to Account	
ACH	Automated Clearing House	ACH
Acquirer	Bank serving merchant in an open loop network	Cards
Ad valorem	Latin for 'according to value'	
ADC	Account Data Compromise	
AeBA	Aadhaar-enabled Bank Account	
AFP	Association for Financial Professionals	
AFS	Alternative Financial Service	
AML	Anti-Money Laundering	
APACS	Association for Payment Clearing Services	
APCA	Australian Payments Clearing Association	
API	Application Programming Interface	
ARC	Account Receivable Conversion; ACH Transaction Code	ACH
ARQC	Authorization Request Cryptogram	
AUP	Acceptable Use Policy	
AVS	Address Verification Services	Cards
B2B	Business to Business	
B2C	Business to Consumer	
BACS	Bankers Automated Clearing Service	
BAN	Bank Account Number	
BBAN	Base Bank Account Number	
BHC	Bank Holding Company	
BIC	Bank Identifier Code	
BIS	Bank of International Settlements	
BLE	Bluetooth Low Energy	
BMO	Bank of Montreal	
BOC	Back Office Conversion; ACH Transaction Code	ACH
BofFD	Bank of First Deposit	Checks
BPS	Basis Points	
BRIC	Brazil, Russia, India, China	
BRL	Brazil Real Currency	
BSA	Bank Secrecy Act	
C2B	Consumer to Business	
C2C	Consumer to Consumer	
CAGR	Compound Annual Growth Rate	
CCD	Corporate Concentration and Disbursement; ACH Transaction Code	ACH
CDMA	Code Division Multiple Access	Cards
CFPB	Consumer Financial Protection Bureau	
CFSI	Center for Financial Services Innovation	
CHAPS	Clearing House Automated Payment System	
Check21	Check Clearing for the 21st Century; a U.S. Federal Law	Checks
CHIPS	Clearing House for International Payments	Wires

Industry Terminology/Acronyms

Term	Definition	Payment System
CNP	Card Not Present	Cards
COF	Cost of Funds	
CP	Card Present	Cards
CRM	Customer Relationship Management	
CTR	Currency Transaction Report	Cash
CTX	Corporate Trade Exchange; ACH Transaction Code	ACH
CU	Credit Union	
CVC	Card Verification Code	Cards
CVC2	Card Validation Check Value	Cards
CVN	Card Verification Number	Cards
CVV	Card Verification Value	Cards
CVV2	Card Verification Value 2	Cards
DB	Deutsche Bank	
DC	Diners Club	Cards
DCC	Dynamic Currency Conversion	Cards
DCT	Depository Check Truncation; ACH Transaction Code	ACH
DDA	Direct Deposit Account; bank checking account	
DDoS	Distributed Denial of Service	
DES	Data Encryption Standard	
DOJ	Department of Justice	
DPAN	Digital Primary Account Number / Device Primary Account Number	Cards
DPS	Debit Processing Service	Cards
DSRP	Digital Secure Remote Payments	Cards
DSS	Data Security Standard	
Duality	i.e. issuers can issue Wells Fargo Visa or Wells Fargo AmEx	
E2E	End-to-End	
E3	End-to-End Encryption	
EACHA	European ACH Association	
EBIT	Earnings Before Interest and Taxes	
EFTA	European Free Trade Association	
EC	European Commission	
ECCHO	Electronic Check Clearing House Organization	Checks
ECOA	Equal Credit Opportunity Act	
ECP	Electronic Check Presentment	Checks
ECRs	Electronic Cash Register	
EDI	Electronic Data Interchange	
EEA	European Economic Area	
EFAA	Expedited Funds Availability Act	
EFT	Electronic Funds Transfer; a general term	
ELV	Elektronisches Lastschriftverfahren – a German term meaning electronic direct debit	
EMV	EuroPay, Mastercard, Visa; chip card standard	Cards
EPO	Electronic Payment Order	
ERP	Enterprise Resource Planning	
ETF	Exchanged Traded Fund	
EWS	Early Warning Systems	
F3X	Fixed-to-fixed (foreign currency to foreign currency) exchange	
FATCA	Foreign Account Tax Compliance Act	
FATF	Financial Action Task Force	
FBAR	Foreign Bank Account Report	
FCRA	Fair Credit Reporting Act	

Industry Terminology/Acronyms

Term	Definition	Payment System
FDIC	Federal Deposit Insurance Corporation	
FF	Fixed-to-fixed (i.e. USD to USD) foreign exchange	
FFIEC	Federal Financial Institution Examination Council	
FHC	Financial Holding Company	
FI	Financial Institution	
Fiat money	Currency that a government has declared to be legal tender, but is not backed by a physical commodity.	
FICO	Fair Isaac Corporation	
FIDO	Fast IDentity Online	
FinCEN	Financial Crimes Enforcement Network	
FinTech	Financial Technology	
FPE	Format Preserving Encryption	
FRB	Federal Reserve Board	
FSN	Financial Services Network	
FV	Fixed-to-variable foreign exchange	
FX	Foreign Exchange	
G2C	Government to Consumer	
GAFI	Groupe d'action financière	
GPR	General Purpose Reloadable (prepaid card)	Cards
GRS	Golden Retriever Systems	Cards
GSM	Global System for Mobile Communications	
GSMA	Groupe Speciale Mobile Association	
HCE	Host Card Emulation	Cards
HSBC	Hongkong and Shanghai Banking Association	
IAT	International ACH Transactions	ACH
IBAN	International Bank Account Number	
IBE	Identity-based Encryption	
ID&V	Identification and Verification	
IFX	Interactive Financial Exchange protocol	
IIN	Issuer Identification Number	
ILCs	Industrial Loan Corporation	
ILP	Interledger Protocol	
IPFA	International Payments Framework Assn.	
IP-POS	Internet Protocol-Point of Sale	Cards
IPO	Initial Public Offering	
IRD	Image Replacement Document	Checks
IRF	Issuer Reimbursement Fee	Cards
ISO	Independent Sales Organization	Cards
IVR	Interactive Voice Response	
JAM Trinity	Jan Dhan Yojana, Aadhaar and Mobile	
JCB	Japan Credit Bureau	Cards
JPMC	JPMorgan Chase	
KBA	Knowledge-Based Authentication	
KYC	Know Your Customer	
LAN	Local Area Network	
LATAM	Latin America Markets	
M&A	Mergers and Acquisitions	
MAU	Monthly Active Users	
MBC	Math-based Currency	
MCC	Merchant Category Code	Cards
MCP	Multi-currency Processing	
MDES	Mastercard Digital Enablement Service	Cards

Industry Terminology/Acronyms

Term	Definition	Payment System
MICR	Magnetic Ink Character Recognition	Checks
MIF	Multilateral Interchange Fees	Cards
MNO	Mobile Network Operator	
MO/TO	Mail Order/Telephone Order	
mPOS	Mobile Point of Sale	
MPSCo	Mobile Payments Service Company Limited	
MSB	Money Service Business	
MST	Magnetic Secure Transmission	Cards
MT	Message Type	
NACHA	NACHA: The Electronic Payments Association	ACH
NCUA	National Credit Union Association	
NFC	Near Field Communication	
NII	Net Interest Income	
NPCI	National Payments Corporation of India	
NPP	New Payments Platform – Australia's low-value, faster payments system	
NRF	National Retail Foundation	
NSF	Non-sufficient Funds	
O/D	Overdraft	
O2O	Offline to Online OR Online to Offline	
OCC	Office of Comptroller of the Currency	
OCT	Original Credit Transaction	Cards
ODFI	Originating Depository Financial Institution	ACH
OEM	Original equipment manufacturer	
OFAC	Office of Foreign Assets Control	
OTA	Over the Air	
OTS	Office of Thrift Supervision	
P2P	Person to Person	
PAG	Payment Access Gateways	
PAR	Payment Account Reference	
PAN	Primary Account Number	Cards
PC	Prepaid Card	
PCE	Personal Consumption Expenditures	
PCI	Payment Card Industry	Cards
PCI-DSS	PCI Data Security Standard	Cards
PE-ACH	PanEuropean ACH	
PFM	Personal Financial Management	
PII	Personally Identifiable Information	
PIN	Personal Identification Number	
PKO	Public Key Infrastructure	
PO	Purchase Order	
POI	Point of Interaction	
POP	Point of Purchase; ACH Transaction Code	ACH
POS	Point of Sale	
PPD	Prearranged Payment and Deposit; ACH Transaction Code	ACH
PSD	Payment Services Directive	
PSD2	Payment Services Directive 2	
PSP	Payments Services Provider	
PTO	Paper Turn-Off	
QSR	Quick Service Restaurant	
RAL	Refund Anticipation Loan	
RCK	Represented Check; ACH Transaction Code	ACH

Industry Terminology/Acronyms

Term	Definition	Payment System
RDC	Remote Deposit Capture	Checks
RDFI	Recipient Depository Financial Institution	ACH
Reg CC	Federal Reserve Bank Regulation	
Reg E	Federal Reserve Bank Regulation	
Reg J	Federal Reserve Bank Regulation	
Reg Z	Federal Reserve Bank Regulation	
RFID	Radio Frequency Identification Device	
RIS	Risk Identification Service	Cards
ROW	Rest of World	
RPPS	Remote Payment and Presentment Service	
RSS	Really Simple Syndication	
RTGS	Real Time Gross Settlement	Wires
RTP	Remittance Transfer Provider	
S&L	Savings & Loan	
SaaS	Software as a Service	
SADC	Southern African Development Community	
SCF	SEPA Cards Framework	
SCT	SEPA Credit Transfer	
SDD B2B	SEPA Direct Debit B2B	
SDD CORE	SEPA Direct Debit Core	
SDK	Software Development Kit	
SE	Secure Element	Cards
SEC	Standard Entry Class Codes	ACH
SECA	Single Euro Cash Area	
SEPA	Single Euro Payments Area	
SKU	Stock Keeping Unit	
SIM	Subscriber Identity Module	
SMB	Small and Medium Business	
SMS	Short Message Service	
SQS	Simple Queue Service	
SSN	Social Security Number	
SSO	Single Sign On	
STE	Secure Token Exchange	
STP	Straight Through Processing	
SVPCo	Small Value Payments Company	
SWIFT	Society for Worldwide Interbank Financial Telecommunication	Wires
"T+2" Funding	Trade date plus 2 days; merchants way to describe a sales transaction that doesn't get cleared/funded for 2 days	
T&E	Travel & Expenses	
TCH	The Clearing House	
TEE	Trusted Execution Environment	
TILA	Truth In Lending Act	
TPV	Total Purchase Volume	
TSM	Trusted Services Manager	Cards
TSP	Token Service Provider	
TSP	Trusted Service Provider	
U2F	User Second Factor	
UAF	Universal Authentication Framework	
UATP	Universal Air Travel Plan	
UCAF	Universal Cardholder Authentication Field	Cards
UCC	Uniform Commercial Code	
UI	User Interface	

Industry Terminology/Acronyms

Term	Definition	Payment System
UIDAI	Unique Identification Authority of India	
UPI	Unified Payments Interface	
UPIC	Universal Payment Identification Code	
UUID	Universally Unique Identifier	
VAN	Value Added Network	ACH
VAR	Value-Added Reseller	
VAT	Value Added Tax	
VbV	Verified by Visa	Cards
VC	Venture Capitalist	
VCN	Visa Commerce Network	Cards
VDC	Virtual Debit Card	Cards
VDEP	Visa Digital Enablement Program	Cards
V/M/D/A	Visa, Mastercard, Discover, American Express	
VMBeacons	Visual Merchandising Beacons	
VTS	Visa Tokenization Service	Cards
W3C	World Wide Web Consortium	
WAEMU	West African Economic and Monetary Union	
XML	Extensible Markup Language	
XRP	Ripple's native, digital currency	
XS2A	Access to Accounts	

Index

banks, 1, 4, 5–7, 9, 10–15, 17–27, 29–45, 47–51, 53–64, 66–74, 76, 77–78, 79, 80, 81, 82, 83, 84, 85, 86, 87, 90, 91, 92, 93, 94, 95, 97–102, 103, 104, 105, 106, 107, 108, 114, 118–121, 122, 123–127, 129, 130, 131–132, 134, 136, 137, 139, 140, 141, 142, 145–153, 159, 160, 169, 170

Bank Secrecy Act, 18, 121

big data, 165

bilateral adoption, 162, 172

biller direct, 140

billers, 18, 40, 43, 57, 58, 62, 84, 91, 98, 129, 135, 139, 140, 141, 151

bill payments, 7, 9, 37, 45, 52, 53, 55, 56, 57, 59, 63, 74, 81, 84, 89, 97, 98, 101, 104, 105, 131, 139, 140, 141, 152

BIN, 77, 108

biometric authentication, 164, 166, 171

Bitcoin, 71, 166

Blackhawk Network, 155, 170

blockchain, 166

BNY/Mellon, 127

BOC, 41, 54

bounced checks, 42, 43

brand, 8, 9, 14, 16, 23, 50, 51, 61, 66, 68, 71, 72, 78, 82, 85, 86, 93, 94, 100, 101, 102, 104, 150, 152

Brinks, 121

broadband, 137

Bureau of Engraving and Printing, 118, 122

Business to Business. *See* B2B

business-to-business transactions. *See* B2B transactions

bust out, 113

C

Capital One, 61, 91, 166

capture, 31, 35, 39, 54, 57, 67, 71, 73, 78, 89, 112

card fees, 96

card issuers, 17, 21, 22, 65, 67, 72, 73, 74, 76, 78, 79, 81, 83, 85, 86, 87, 89, 91, 94, 95, 97, 99, 100, 105, 109, 110, 111, 112, 113, 114, 115, 121, 135, 140, 141, 148, 152, 158, 160

card-not-present. *See* CNP

cards, 1, 2, 5, 7, 8, 10, 11, 16, 17, 18, 25, 26, 31, 35, 36, 41, 48, 57, 61, 65, 67, 68, 69, 71, 72, 73, 74, 75, 76, 77, 78, 79, 80, 81, 82, 83, 84, 85, 86, 89, 90, 91, 92, 93, 94, 95, 96, 97, 98, 99, 100,

101, 102, 103, 104, 105, 111, 112, 113, 114, 115, 122, 130, 131, 132, 133, 134, 135, 136, 138, 139, 140, 147, 148, 150, 152, 155, 156, 158, 159, 160, 162, 168, 169, 170

Cardtronics, 121

Card Verification Code. *See* CVC

Card Verification Value. *See* CVV

cash, 7, 8, 14, 15, 21, 27, 30, 33, 39, 41, 44, 68, 73, 81, 82, 98, 99, 102, 104, 115, 117, 118, 119, 120, 121, 122, 130, 131, 132, 133, 134, 139, 141, 151, 158, 159, 163

cash letters, 34, 37

cash management, 142, 147

CCD Credit, 53

CCD Debit, 53

central banks, 25, 27

certified checks, 29, 41

Chain of Liability, 5, 6

chargebacks, 92, 108, 109

charge cards, 65, 72, 74, 76, 82, 84, 91, 93, 94, 95, 110

charters, 146

Check 21, 17, 32, 33, 36, 44

check cashing, 41, 130, 131, 152

check clearing houses, 7, 17, 23, 29, 30, 35, 36, 37, 43, 48, 50, 147

check conversion, 43, 53, 54

check fraud, 42, 43, 44, 141

check guarantee service, 41

checking accounts, 19, 29, 33, 38, 67, 68, 69, 72, 73, 91, 95, 96, 98, 99, 100, 101, 102, 104, 120, 131, 139, 142, 145, 146, 147, 149, 160, 161, 170

checking system, 7, 10, 14, 29, 30, 31, 34, 38, 43

check kiting, 42

check verification, 43, 44

chip cards, 78, 79, 112

CHIPS, 15, 16, 45, 123, 125, 126, 127, 128

Citibank, 91, 127

Clearing House Interbank Payments System. *See* CHIPS

clearing houses, 5, 7, 9, 10, 14, 17, 23, 27, 29, 30, 31, 32, 34, 35, 36, 37, 42, 43, 44, 45, 47, 48, 50, 61, 63, 123, 125, 128, 129, 145, 147, 151

closed loop, 4, 6, 7, 9, 13, 15, 19, 23, 25, 65, 73, 75, 84, 90, 94, 102, 103, 104, 105, 117, 150, 152

closed loop payments system, 6, 25, 150

M

machine learning, 149, 164, 165, 168
magnetic ink character recognition.
   See MICR
magnetic stripes, 69, 77, 78, 79, 80, 92,
   99, 112, 113, 156, 168
marketplaces, 91, 166, 167
Mastercard, 9, 15, 16, 23, 61, 66, 67,
   68, 69, 70, 72, 73, 74, 78, 83, 89, 95,
   96, 100, 101, 115, 136, 150, 151, 169
Mastercard WorldCard, 95
merchant coalitions, 90
merchant discount fees, 61, 62, 87, 88,
   89, 90, 94, 101, 108, 109, 136, 153
merchants, 2, 4, 12, 18, 22, 23, 40, 41,
   43, 52, 56, 58, 59, 62, 67, 69, 71, 73,
   74, 76, 78, 79, 81, 82, 83, 84, 88, 89,
   90, 91, 92, 94, 97, 98, 101, 103, 105,
   106, 107, 109, 110, 111, 113, 114,
   118, 119, 130, 134, 135, 136, 137,
   138, 140, 141, 143, 151, 152, 153,
   162, 165, 170, 171, 172
MICR, 31, 32, 36, 40, 41, 47, 54
mobile, 1, 7, 9, 39, 57, 64, 71, 80, 98,
   114, 115, 119, 130, 131, 132, 133,
   135, 137, 138, 146, 148, 149, 158,
   159, 162, 164, 165, 166, 167, 168
mobile commerce, 138
mobile payments, 64, 80, 130, 131, 135,
   137, 138, 158, 162
Money Center Banks, 127
MoneyGram, 152
MoneyPass, 121
money transmitters, 18
MOTO, 136
M-Pesa, 119, 171
multilateral netting, 125

N

NAAIO, 122
NACHA, 16, 27, 35, 41, 47, 50, 51, 52,
   53, 56, 57, 60, 61, 62, 63, 64, 101
National Settlement Service, 44, 49
NCR, 121
Near Field Communication. *See* NFC
negotiable instruments, 29
net settlement, 12, 14, 27, 30, 34, 49,
   61, 85, 123
networks, 5, 6, 9, 10, 11, 12, 14, 15, 16,
   18, 19, 21, 22, 23, 25, 26, 27, 29, 47,
   48, 50, 53, 57, 59, 61, 62, 65, 67, 68,
   69, 70, 71, 72, 73, 74, 75, 76, 77, 78,
   79, 80, 81, 82, 83, 84, 85, 86, 87, 88,
   89, 90, 91, 92, 94, 95, 96, 97, 98, 99,

100, 101, 102, 104, 105, 106, 108,
   109, 110, 111, 112, 113, 114, 115,
   117, 119, 120, 121, 123, 124, 126,
   127, 129, 137, 138, 140, 141, 145,
   147, 150, 151, 152, 153, 155, 156,
   158, 159, 160, 163, 164, 166, 169,
   170
NFC, 71, 80, 138
Non-sufficient Funds. *See* NSF
NSF, 12, 21, 27, 38, 42, 43, 56, 58, 99,
   101, 102
NYCE, 15, 50, 68, 70, 74, 100

O

OCC, 146
ODFI, 49, 54, 55, 56, 57, 58, 60, 61
Office of the Comptroller of the
   Currency. *See* OCC
on-us, 5, 24, 31, 56, 60, 127, 153
open loop, 4, 5, 6, 7, 9, 10, 12, 15, 16,
   19, 20, 21, 22, 24, 26, 29, 104, 122,
   127, 134, 150
open source software, 165
operations risk, 22
Oracle, 121
order ahead, 162
Originating Depository Financial
   Institution. *See* ODFI
originator, 49, 54, 55, 56, 57, 58, 60
overdraft fees, 19, 20, 99, 149
overdrafts, 42, 99

P

P2P payments, 9, 52, 57, 131, 133, 171
PaaS, 71, 113, 137
PAN, 77, 78, 96
paper turn off. *See* PTO
PATRIOT Act of 2001, 98
paying banks, 32, 34, 35, 36, 42, 43
Payment Alliance, 121
Payment Card Industry. *See* PCI
Payments as a Service. *See* PaaS
payments services providers, 6, 7, 21,
   25, 57, 129, 152, 153
payments system economics, 18, 19
payments systems, 2, 3, 4, 5, 6, 7, 8, 9,
   10, 12, 13, 14, 15, 16, 17, 18, 19, 20,
   21, 22, 23, 24, 25, 26, 27, 29, 30, 31,
   32, 33, 36, 37, 44, 45, 48, 49, 52, 61,
   62, 63, 65, 66, 76, 84, 89, 103, 114,
   117, 122, 123, 124, 126, 127, 129,
   130, 133, 135, 141, 143, 145, 149,
   150, 151, 153, 156, 161, 163, 167,
   171, 172

PayPal, 7, 23, 25, 56, 57, 71, 110, 152, 155, 157, 159, 160–161, 169, 172, 173

payroll, 11, 38, 41, 48, 50, 52, 53, 58, 59, 104, 105, 131, 142

payroll cards, 104, 131

PCI, 83, 113, 114, 137

PCI Data Security Standard. *See* PCI-DSS

PCI-DSS, 22, 34, 71, 83, 112, 113, 114, 137, 138, 156

personal identification number. *See* PIN

person-to-person payments. *See* P2P payments

Philadelphia Federal Reserve Bank Payments Card Center, 115

PIN, 12, 16, 23, 27, 69, 70, 73, 74, 76, 79, 80, 81, 82, 84, 89, 90, 96, 97, 100, 101, 113, 119

PIN debit, 16, 23, 69, 70, 73, 74, 76, 81, 82, 84, 89, 90, 96, 97, 100, 101, 113, 119

PIN debit network, 69, 70, 73, 74, 96

point of purchase. *See* POP

point of sale. *See* POS

POP, 41, 54

POS, 1, 9, 37, 45, 52, 54, 56, 59, 61, 64, 67, 69, 71, 73, 76, 79, 80, 81, 89, 91, 92, 96, 97, 98, 101, 106, 107, 114, 115, 119, 120, 122, 130, 131, 134, 137, 138, 147, 160, 162, 166, 169, 170

positive pay, 39, 143

POS terminals, 67, 71, 76, 79, 89, 106, 107

PPD Credit, 52

PPD Debit, 52, 53, 60

prepaid cards, 7, 8, 25, 48, 71, 73, 81, 91, 93, 102, 103, 104, 105, 111, 121, 122, 133, 134, 152, 155, 162, 169, 170

presentment, 32, 34, 37, 59, 139

Primary Account Number. *See* PAN

private label cards, 75, 94, 135

processing, 8, 9, 16, 19, 20, 22, 23, 24, 27, 29, 30, 31, 32, 35, 36, 37, 38, 42, 44, 45, 47, 50, 60, 61, 62, 63, 65, 68, 69, 72, 73, 76, 77, 79, 81, 85, 86, 93, 97, 98, 100, 101, 102, 103, 105, 107, 108, 109, 113, 123, 126, 134, 137, 146, 147, 150, 151, 152, 153

processors, 1, 9, 15, 17, 18, 22, 23, 29, 31, 34, 35, 36, 42, 44, 58, 60, 62, 63, 65, 70, 71, 74, 75, 76, 77, 80, 81, 84,

93, 99, 100, 103, 105, 107, 108, 112, 113, 114, 121, 129, 140, 142, 145, 146, 150, 151, 152, 153

PTO, 140

push payments, 11, 61, 168

Q

QuickBooks, 41

R

Radio Frequency Identification Device. *See* RFID

RDC, 10, 39, 40, 41, 42, 43

RDFIs, 49, 51, 53, 57, 58, 59, 60, 61, 63

real-time gross settlement. *See* RTGS

recurring bill payments, 53, 131

Regulation CC, 17, 33

Regulation E, 17, 51, 53, 105

Regulation J, 17

Regulation Z, 17, 84

relationships, 4, 5, 7, 18, 25, 67, 68, 95, 101, 132, 142, 145, 148, 153, 166

remittance data, 10, 39, 53, 57, 59, 127, 143

remote deposit capture. *See* RDC

reputation risk, 22

retail lockbox, 39, 59

rewards, 1, 71, 89, 91, 92, 94, 95, 98, 99, 101, 102, 130, 131, 132, 133, 135, 136, 158

rewards programs, 94, 95, 98, 99, 101, 115, 133

RFID, 79

risk management, 2, 21, 23, 26, 29, 42, 44, 47, 53, 57, 60, 62, 65, 75, 83, 85, 98, 107, 110, 111, 121, 123, 125, 126, 134, 141, 148

risks, 1, 2, 10, 12, 16, 21, 22, 23, 24, 26, 27, 29, 32, 38, 40, 42, 43, 44, 45, 47, 48, 49, 53, 55, 56, 57, 58, 60, 61, 62, 64, 65, 69, 73, 74, 75, 83, 85, 96, 97, 98, 101, 102, 107, 109, 110, 111, 113, 121, 123, 125, 126, 134, 135, 136, 137, 140, 141, 143, 148, 151, 153, 157, 158, 159, 165, 172

RTGS, 123, 125

rules, 3, 5, 6, 8, 9, 12, 13, 14, 15, 16, 17, 22, 23, 25, 26, 27, 29, 35, 37, 41, 44, 47, 51, 52, 53, 55, 57, 62, 63, 65, 66, 67, 72, 73, 74, 75, 76, 77, 78, 82, 83, 84, 85, 86, 90, 92, 96, 97, 100, 101, 105, 108, 109, 110, 111, 113, 117, 123, 126, 137, 141, 150, 151, 156, 159, 163, 169, 170

Want to learn more about payments? Glenbrook's Payments Industry Education Program is designed to help payment professionals reach new levels of understanding into the payments industry.

Glenbrook's Payments Boot Camps and Private Payments Workshops are comprehensive, covering industry topics from "soup to nuts." We cover business structure and economics, market positions and strategies, technology, regulation, operations, and risk management. We discuss current trends and issues and place both into the context of current industry practices.

Glenbrook Payments Industry Education

Glenbrook Payments Boot Camp

- Glenbrook's popular Payments Boot Camp is a two-day "deep dive" into the payments industry, covering the basics of the industry, current issues, and the emerging FinTech landscape.
- The agenda is structured to ensure that you understand how the industry works as a whole. Day 1 emphasizes industry fundamentals and the dynamics between stakeholders. Day 2 focuses on the impact of technology and how the industry is changing.
- Glenbrook Payments Boot Camps are held regularly in the San Francisco Bay Area and in New York City.

Private Payments Workshops

- Let us bring our experts to your location. A Private Payments Workshop gives you a unique opportunity to expand your team's knowledge of the payments industry.
- The agenda for each workshop is customized to fit the needs of your organization. We start with material from Glenbrook's flagship Payments Boot Camp and can adjust agenda topics and topics depth.
- Private Payments Workshops are one-day, two-day, or three-day sessions.

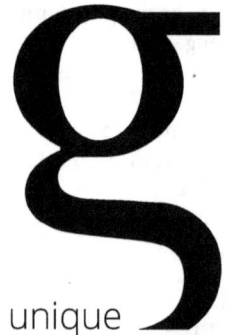

Through this unique Payments Industry Education Program, Glenbrook shares its experience and insights with payments professionals eager to understand industry fundamentals and how they are evolving.

For more information on Glenbrook's Payments Industry Education program and to see the current workshop schedule, visit our website at **www.glenbrook.com**. For information on scheduling a Private Payments Workshop, please contacts us at **bootcamp@glenbrook.com**.

g GLENBROOK

www.ingramcontent.com/pod-product-compliance
Lightning Source LLC
Chambersburg PA
CBHW081524220326
41598CB00036B/6321